MEADOWLARK

MEADOWLARK

MEADOWLARK LEMON

WITH

JERRY B. JENKINS

THOMAS NELSON PUBLISHERS
Nashville • Camden • Kansas City

Copyright © 1987 by Meadowlark Lemon and Jerry Jenkins

Published in Nashville, Tennessee, by Thomas Nelson, Inc., and distributed in Canada by Lawson Falle, Ltd., Cambridge, Ontario.

Printed in the United States of America.

ISBN 0-8407-4220-7

1 2 3 4 5 6—91 90 89 88 87

*To the millions all over the world
who enjoyed the Harlem Globetrotters,
the Bucketeers, and the Shooting Stars,
and who let us know it.*

Contents

Acknowledgments

Special thanks to Sherry Fischer, Lorelei Lemon, Shirley Moore of the Wilmington (North Carolina) *Morning Star,* and our editor, Janet Hoover Thoma, who did so much more than just edit.

MEADOWLARK

1

The Birth of a Dream

The course of my life was set when I was eleven years old. It happened in a movie theater of all places.

At the Ritz in my hometown of Wilmington, North Carolina, you could watch everything all day for twenty five cents. That included the Movietone newsreel, the cartoons, the short features, and the action serials. Growing up in the 1940s, I lived for the changing of the movies, but if they hadn't changed in a couple of days, I paid and watched the same feature again.

One Saturday my friends and I got up early and headed to the bakery for a supply of Washington pies. We planned to spend the entire day at the Ritz, and popcorn couldn't satisfy our hunger. Washington pies were made from stale bread that had been softened with water and sprinkled with sugar, then cooked like bread pudding. If we had enough money, we would get one with apple bits in it or even with icing. Washington pies were heavy and thick and cheap.

I put mine in my pocket, just in case I ran into anyone who thought I looked gangly enough to intimidate. Often the older kids, particularly a guy named Red Sumpter, waited at the head of the line at the Ritz, ready to take our popcorn money or any food we brought with us. We had to have enough for ourselves and for them, or we wound up giving them our admission money and then having to sneak in.

My buddies—Edward "Nerves" Sutton and Gene "Flick" Black—and I tried that a lot, but the owner knew us since we sometimes helped him sell programs. So, when we sneaked in the back door and picked up ticket stubs to pretend we had paid, he ran us out. "Meadow, Sutton, Flick, let's go. You didn't pay today."

That Saturday we purposely got to the Ritz early, before the older guys, and got our popcorn and RC Colas. Then we settled in for a long day.

It was about nine in the morning. The features would start rolling in less than an hour, and my dad said I had to be home by eight. I had enough food to last me, and I was with my friends. Eleven hours of fun! We might see Tex Ritter, Gene Autry, Buck Jones, Johnny Mack Brown, the Lone Ranger, or Superman, a couple of black comedies with Pigmeat Markham or Steppin' Fetchit, maybe some jazz with Dizzie Gillespie or Cab Calloway, and three or four cartoons.

There would also be newsreels, but they didn't interest us much. Even though this was our only way to get world news since we didn't have radio or TV, we were usually horsing around when the newsreel told the latest about President Roosevelt and the war.

Half our snacks were gone by the time the Ritz was full and the lights went down. That was the signal for hooting and hollering, but when the cartoons started, everybody shut up, except for laughing.

The movies had been running for a little over half an hour that Saturday morning. I was probably as content as a kid could be in those days. I had my fears and my troubles, but basically I was happy. I had no idea that within the next few minutes, my life would change forever.

Kids were throwing popcorn and pinching each other when the Movietone newsreel began, but there was something different about this one. As soon as the theme music faded, the tune started that would be the background for the short news feature. The word *Harlem* caught my ear because that was where my mother lived.

And what was this? A bunch of tall black men in a locker room, lacing up their shoes, singing together. I leaned forward. I was aware of nothing but that music and those black men who seemed to be having so much fun together.

The newsreel was in black and white, of course, but as the announcer talked about the Harlem Globetrotters and their red, blue, and white uniforms, I could see the colors. He mentioned their names: Rookie Brown, Duke Cumberland, Sweetwater Clifton, and Goose Tatum.

I could hardly stay in my seat with that jumpin', jivin', whistlin' music blaring. It made you want to dance, and that's what these guys, these Harlem Globetrotters, were doing. Smiling, singing, slapping each other on the back, tumbling from the locker room to a basketball court, a big one with thousands of fans in the stands.

The first thing they did was the "Magic Circle," passing the ball to each other, faking, mugging, dancing to the music of "Sweet Georgia Brown." What they could do with that ball! And Goose Tatum! He looked like his arms and legs weren't even attached to his body.

He pranced and strutted his stuff, smiling, laughing, carrying on. And how they could play! They flew up and down the court, passing, dribbling, shooting, rebounding. My heart raced. My head nearly ached. I couldn't believe what I was seeing.

The athletic ability was fantastic, of course, but there was something else. It was the joy, the teamwork, the sense of family. It was the most wonderful thing I had ever seen in my life. It was grown men—black men—who still had buddies they played with.

It was only a short feature, but it crashed in on my senses. I stared, not blinking, hardly breathing. In a flash, I knew I wanted to be on that team, the Harlem Globetrotters. I didn't know anything but their names and their song, and I had never seen a basketball or a hoop, but I was going to be a Harlem Globetrotter and that was final.

I couldn't even tell my friends, it was so real and dynamic and personal. As soon as the newsreel ended, I leaped from my seat and raced up the aisle. "Slim, where you goin', man? The feature's comin' on next!"

An adult voice said, "Don't be runnin' in the theater, Meadow!"

I couldn't slow down. I bounded through the little lobby, past the concession stand, and through the door. "Hey, slow down in here! You leave, you can't come back without payin' again!"

None of that mattered. I had had a life-changing experience, and I knew it. I had to find my dad, but as I raced home, I couldn't remember if he was at work, out gambling, sleeping, or what.

I burst through the door of his house and hollered for him. No one was there. I spun around, unable to control myself. I was whistling "Sweet Georgia Brown" and running those names over and over in my head. *Rookie Brown, Duke Cumberland, Sweetwater Clifton, Goose Tatum—and, someday, Meadow Lemon!*

I had to learn the game, find out where that team was from in Harlem, and get ready for my career. It never occurred to me that I had wasted my admission money for just a few cartoons and a newsreel. Deep inside I knew that somehow that experience was worth everything I owned.

Where was Dad? I just had to tell him. I rummaged around in the kitchen cupboard and found an onion sack with only a couple of onions left. I dumped them out, tore the paper away from the middle of the netting, and cut the bottom off the sack. In an upstairs closet I found a hanger, which I pulled apart on my way back downstairs.

Carrying a hammer and huge nails, I crossed the street and climbed the big tree next to the Robinsons. I don't know how I did it, balancing on one huge limb, but somehow I threaded that onion bag net onto the hanger, bent the hanger into sort of a circle, and nailed the whole mess to the trunk of the tree, maybe eight or nine feet off the ground.

I tossed the hammer down and dropped to the ground. What would I do for a ball? Everyone I knew that might have one was at the Ritz and would be there all day. I took the hammer back to my dad's house and dug through the garbage. An empty Carnation Evaporated Milk can was as close as I could come to anything round.

I ran back across the street. Needless to say, the can wouldn't bounce. I tried to remember how the Globetrotters held the ball and shot it. I wound up throwing it like a baseball toward the basket. About every ten shots, one miraculously dropped through.

Finally, my dad arrived home. I ran over and met him at the door, talking so fast no one would have been able to understand. I don't think he knew what hit him. "Dad! Dad! I know what I want to be when I grow up. A Harlem Globetrotter! It's a basketball team! They're great. They sing and dance and play basketball, and there's Duke and Rookie and Sweetwater and Goose, and I'm gonna be one!"

Dad smiled and shook his head. "Movies over already?"

"I gotta practice! Watch!" I tried shooting the can again but had no more luck than before. Once the can hit the net, and the hoop came down. I told Dad to wait and watch again, but when I looked across the street, he'd already gone into the house. That was all right. I couldn't blame him. It was frustrating to watch the can hit the rim or the tree, but I knew I'd get it right someday.

When the rest of the guys finally got back from the Ritz that night, I was still out there shooting that evaporated milk can. I hadn't improved one iota. One guy got the idea of trying a softball, then a tennis ball, and pretty soon we were all playing. None of us were any good, but I was going to be. I'd work at it, I'd give myself to it. I'd learn this game, find out what it was all about, and do whatever I could to become a Harlem Globetrotter.

Nothing else mattered.

2

Peanut Lemon

My dad was known as the gambler's gambler—at least he thought so—and he carried a switchblade knife, set halfway open with a small piece of match stick so the handle dangled outside his pocket. Legend says he was so fast with that thing that once, when a man in a card game drew down on him with a forty-five, Dad had that blade out and snapped open at the man's throat before he could blink.

Dad was tough. You didn't mess with him. I saw quite a bit of my dad, even though my parents had divorced when I was a pre-schooler, and I, their only child, had been sent to live with my Aunt Maggie and Uncle Frank and their seven children. We lived in a tiny house that was also home to a couple of my dad's brothers and his mother.

My dad lived a block and a half west at Sixth and Bladen with his common-law wife. The locals named this black section of Wilmington, "Brooklyn," to identify with the sprawling, exciting New York City borough, probably because most of them dreamed of getting there someday.

Dad kept close track of me, and sometimes I even helped him in his job with the Wilmington Waste Paper and Recycling Company. When Aunt Maggie or Grandma or the other kids made me angry, I'd pack everything I owned in my pillowcase and head up the street to visit Dad for a day or two.

Even though he and Mom were divorced and it was clear someone—perhaps he himself—thought it was better that I not live with him permanently as a child, I still idolized him. Peanut Lemon—he was actually Meadow Lemon II, and I'm Meadow Lemon III—was a short, wiry man with a lot of friends.

And Dad loved me. He wasn't big on saying so, but I knew. He made it as obvious as he could. I had to be only five or six when he proved he would die for me if necessary. That's a lesson that stays on a kid's mind forever.

We were on the run, crossing a busy street, when I stumbled and fell. A car was speeding toward me, and Dad could have easily made it to safety. Instead, he planted his feet and dove back over me as the car screeched to a stop, inches from him. If either of us was going to get it, he was going to be first.

I was weepy and rubbery legged when we got up and hurried off, and it was only after I grew up and had children of my own that I knew how he must have felt.

Wilmington—on the Cape Fear River and not far from the Atlantic in the southeast corner of North Carolina—was a town of forty to fifty thousand back then. Our Brooklyn was a city within a city, a country within a country. It was a place white people drove by or drove through, but they didn't really see. Blacks who could find work got the lowest jobs available on the railroad, in the shipyards, in the pulpwood or chemical plants, or on the docks as longshoremen.

Like anyone else, I wanted out, but not because I didn't love my family and friends. I admit I thought it would be nice to get away from our Little Brooklyn when my cousins or my grandmother had gotten on my nerves or I had just grown tired of not really having a home. I missed my mother, who had moved to 129th Street in New York City's Harlem. She was a beautiful woman who went to New York to be a model, did some modeling, and wound up working in a hotel for several decades. I visited her during the summers, taking a train north to New York and staying in Harlem until the weather turned cold. Then I knew it was time to head back to Wilmington for the school year. My home with Mother was temporary.

One of the saddest days of my life came a little more than ten years ago when I found out that, before she remarried, my mother had written to my dad from New York in an attempt to get back together with him. A neighbor lady received the letter, read it, thought it would cause more trouble than it was worth, and destroyed it. She never told my dad about it. I had always accepted a broken home as my fate, but when I learned of that letter, I ached to think of what might have been. The pain must have been deeper than I realized when I was young.

Everybody in our neighborhood of Brooklyn had funny ways of walking or talking or playing sports. And most of us had nicknames. My family called me Junior, my friends called me Slim, and my enemies called me names I can't put on paper.

The most colorful character in the neighborhood was Richard Gillyard. We called him Son; I don't know why. John Titus, we called Tiptoe, because of the way he walked. I can see John Titus tiptoin' around like it was yesterday. Edward Sutton was called Nerves, because he had developed a series of twitches. And William Boyd was a smallish kid we called Bap because he ran with an older kid named Pap. Lastly, there was Joe Harris, whom we called Thusalem. Even though he was younger than we were, he had the athletic skills of someone much older.

Shoot, we had a better gang than the Little Rascals. We called ourselves the Hometown Boys.

Football was our game. It was a man's game, brutal with lots of contact. Once a game started, guys came from all over the area. As long as the sides were even, we let everyone play. I remember games with as many as twenty on a side. We had one interesting rule: Nothing was out of bounds.

We usually started playing two-hand touch, but then the arguments started. "You only got me with one hand!"

All right, you'd think, *next time he'll feel both hands*. And he did. Then came the challenge, usually from Son, who was known for trying anything. "Let's play tackle and forget this two-hand touch stuff! Touch is for sissies, just like basketball!"

Ironically, basketball was one game we didn't play. I literally didn't know what it was before I saw that Globetrotter newsreel. I'd heard kids talk about basketball being for sissies, but I had never seen a backboard or a hoop, let alone a basketball. They played it at a Boys' Club on the south side of town, way past where I had ever been. That was all I knew about it.

Before I saw the antics of the Globetrotter players, football was enough for me. We ran all over the neighborhood, behind cars, up on porches, over fences, around houses. But when you went around a house to catch a pass, you might find ten guys waiting to knock your head off. Eventually, you had to get back to where the goal line was, and the farther you ran to avoid contact, the more guys there were waiting for you. I still bear the scars from playing those games!

As a sixth grader, I walked all the way to and from Little Williston School every day because that saved me a nickel in bus fare each way. I also helped my dad on his job sometimes after school because he always gave me a little money.

One afternoon he expected me to help, but I didn't show up. When he and his brother Washington—we called him Uncle Wash—got to Aunt Maggie's for dinner that night, Dad was worried. "Is Meadow here?"

Grandma and Aunt Maggie assured him I was but that Dad had better talk to me in private. "Police brought 'im home, Peanut."

"Why? Wha'd he do?" They nodded toward the back porch. I sat out there in the dark, sniffling. My dad sat beside me and turned my chin toward the light. The pain from his touching my battered face made me cry.

He winced. "What happened, boy?"

Between sobs the story spilled out. Three big boys had hassled me on the way to school, but I outran them. On the way home they ambushed me. "Police finally found me lyin' there."

"Who was they, Meadow. You know 'em?"

I nodded. "I know the fat one. Ever'body call him Titty Boo."

Dad asked, "Did you get in any good licks?"

I shook my head. "The other two held me down while Titty Boo punched and kicked me."

Dad had heard enough. He trembled with rage. Still looking at me, he hollered, "Washington! Come out here!"

Uncle Wash must have been standing in the doorway, he was there so fast. He bent down to look at me and let out a low whistle.

Dad spoke softly but with intensity. "You ever hear of a boy name Titty Boo?"

Uncle Wash dragged his hand across his mouth. "Big fat boy?"

Dad nodded.

"Yeah. I know dat boy. He do this?"

Dad nodded again.

Uncle Wash said, "I'm ready, Peanut. Lead the way."

And they went looking for Titty Boo and his friends. Word spread fast because suddenly anyone who had ever known or seen or even heard of Titty Boo was nowhere to be found. We heard later that he and his friends had found out that Peanut and Washington Lemon were looking for them and they left town. I didn't see Titty Boo again for a couple of years, but I'll tell you about that later.

Once Dad found out that I didn't ride the bus because I didn't have the money, he started letting me work with him more often to earn spending money. He also started thinking about having me move down the street with him permanently, but that didn't happen until a year or so later when Aunt Maggie and her family moved to South Carolina.

I rode the bus for the next few weeks, just in case, but I got brave again when I needed more pocket change for the movies. Going to the Ritz with Tiptoe, Bap, Thusalem, Flick, Nerves, and all the guys was sure better than going with Dad to the Bijou, where blacks had to sit up in the balcony.

Dad was embarrassing at the movies. He believed whatever he saw on the screen. He figured if we could hear Johnny Mack Brown or Gene Autry, then they could hear us, too. Right at the moment when everybody in the theater was holding their breath as the villain sneaked up behind the hero, you could count on my dad hollering, "Look out, Johnny! He's right behind you, man!"

By walking to school and helping my dad, it became easier to get the thirty-five cents I needed for a comfortable day at the Ritz and all the food I needed. I even had an extra nickel in case Red Sumpter came looking for me. When I got there early and avoided him in the ticket line, he often came strolling around between features looking for me. I was a skinny dude then, but I hoped one day to tangle with him and put him in his place.

3

Earl Jackson's Hook Shot

The impact of the Harlem Globetrotters on me was magic. In an instant, I had new heroes. I had idolized cowboys like Gene Autry and Tex Ritter, and I knew which one wore his guns backward and which one chewed gum and why. Even though we kids fought over which of us would be which hero when we played every day, we couldn't really identify with them.

For all we knew, all real cowboys were white. If we saw a black cowboy on the screen, it was in a comedy, or he was being played for a fool. We never said we wanted to grow up and be cowboys; down deep we thought we knew better. From studying a little history, I know now that there were just as many black cowboys as white in the Old West.

The Harlem Globetrotters gave me new life, something to strive for. There was not only their togetherness and their music, but they *entertained* people. They made their fans laugh and cheer. Could anything, any job be more wonderful than that? I couldn't get over it. They were black men. Someday I would be a black man. And a Globetrotter.

I never stopped to consider the cost. It was irrelevant. I knew I had a lot to learn. It didn't cross my mind that if God hadn't blessed me with unusually long arms and legs, huge hands, and an eventual height of six three, I might not have had a chance. My sights were set, my goal established. All I knew at that age was that I would have to start logging some time on a basketball court, and there wasn't one close.

I didn't have to tell my friends how deeply I had been affected. They saw it in how I acted, what I said, what I wanted to do all the time. Play basketball. We still did kids' stuff, of course. I was young enough to enjoy playing cowboys and Indians, but I started noticing different things. Kids I used to idolize, ones I had put on pedestals because they were bigger or older or could tell a good joke, began to slide on my most-favored list.

One of the guys, Willie Green, was the best storyteller in the neighborhood. He had a cousin named Daniel who kept his head shaved. I thought those two guys were the coolest on earth. They would hang around playing the dozens, a game where you see how much you can cut down the other guy's family. They made up such outlandish stories that crowds would gather to laugh and howl.

One day, leaving the Ritz, we were arguing over who got to be Tex Ritter, and baldheaded Daniel won. To top it all off, they wouldn't let us younger kids play, so we just watched. They had wooden horses and reins and guns and everything, and they were really going at it. At one point, Daniel-Tex came riding around the house, and one of the crooks bopped him on his bald head with a pistol.

The scalp was laid open, blood was rushing, and Daniel was out. When he came to, he was crying and carrying on. They had to get him to the doctor. He was all right, but it sure made an impression on me. I was astounded. I thought those guys were so adultlike, older than us, bigger than us, cooler than us. And there was ol' Daniel, hurt and crying just like I would have been.

I was growing up, and I didn't even know it.

The division between the races was becoming clearer to me, too. Just a few paces from my dad's house was a white middle school, right in the center of the all-black Brooklyn area of Wilmington. I don't know if it had a gym, since we weren't allowed to enter, but it had a huge playground, enclosed by a brick wall and a fence, which was also off limits.

When the school day was over, we snuck in there, of course. Our softballs and footballs broke a few windows, and when a ball landed on the roof, we shimmied up the downspouts. It's a wonder no one was killed on those rickety things. The police ran us out whenever they saw us on the playground, and that was frequently.

As we got older, we got bolder, and we threw stones at the police cars just to get them to chase us. We knew it was wrong, but we also felt it was wrong to run us off what we thought should have been a public playground right in our own neighborhood. It made us angry. We never tried to hurt anybody or anything, and we weren't quite brave enough to really risk getting caught, but being chased by the police was a little diversion in an otherwise tough existence. We suspected the cops enjoyed the activity, too.

Often as we sat joking out on that brick wall, a squad car would pull by slowly, as if to warn us not to drop down the other side into the school yard. We always waited until dark, when the coast was clear, but someone had to stand guard. If he yelled that the cops were coming, we jumped the six-foot wall and ran between houses all over the neighborhood. The nearly nightly chase was almost as much fun as playing ball.

It was around this time that Aunt Maggie and Uncle Frank moved to South Carolina with their seven kids and whoever else in the family wanted to go. I liked the idea of living with Dad at Sixth and Bladen because that was so close to the Ritz and the school yard and the store where I bought my snacks.

I missed Aunt Maggie's cooking, but I was developing such an appetite, I needed the junk food anyway. It seemed like all we did was play ball, go to the movies, go to school, run from the cops, and sing. And that singing got me my last good whipping from my dad. I'll never forget it.

It wasn't that he didn't know I liked to sing with the guys. He didn't know that I sneaked out my bedroom window and hung out with them after I was supposed to be in bed. When he caught me one night, he took the belt to me and lectured me about amounting to something in life. He really believed that a boy who couldn't find anything better to do than to hang out with a bunch of harmonizing kids would never amount to much. He wanted me to start looking forward to college someday, and singing on a street corner after bedtime was no way to achieve that.

He talked a lot about college, but I wasn't thinking about that. I mean, I was just barely out of sixth grade! I was thinking about going right from high school to the Trotters. I didn't know how you went about that, but college wasn't part of the plan.

I was frustrated, though. There wasn't going to be any Globetrotters for Meadow Lemon III unless I started to really learn basketball. Using a tennis ball was better than using an evaporated milk can, but our hoop was pathetic. I dreamed of how the Globetrotters dribbled and passed and shot and rebounded. They were graceful and fast and fluid. We were slow and uncertain, and the ground was uneven. No one knew how to do anything in the game.

Then the rumors started. The Boys' Club that had been so far south might be moving to the old USO building not far from us. It was too good to be true, but every other day the story changed. We'd get our hopes up, only to have them dashed by a new rumor. I wandered down to that building. It sure was small. What could they make of it? I peeked in the windows. It was dingy and musty.

More than anyone, I wanted that Boys' Club to move there, but there weren't even backboards. Would they have basketballs? All I could do was dream and hope. My vision never faded, but I was eager to get rolling.

It took about a year—the longest year of my life—but eventually someone cut through the red tape, and the USO building was given to the community. A lot of guys showed up the first few days it was open, but it wasn't too popular right after that because all they had were some worn-out old basketballs and a few other things to play with. Still, I got my hands on a real basketball. It was limp and underinflated, but I got the feel of it.

I bounced it on the floor, and it came back up to me. I smacked it, and it bounced away. I knew it would be better with a little air, but it would be a few weeks before anyone pumped up the balls. I just tossed it in the air and ran around, banging it off the walls, getting used to how it bounced and anticipating where to catch it.

When the balls were inflated, they were a lot more fun, but I had to retrain myself. The basketball was much more lively, and I found it difficult to learn to dribble. By then I had seen older kids play here and there, and they were able to dribble and pass and shoot without looking at the ball all the time. That took me weeks to perfect, but I had the time because there were no baskets to distract me.

Watching those baskets finally go up was like having a ringside seat to eternity. I wondered if they'd ever start, and I knew they would never finish. The crated backboards were delivered by truck and sat there for several days. Every time I made the ten-minute walk, I prayed that the backboards would be up. They weren't.

Finally, I saw some men from the city there with tools. I watched as they drilled holes and hoisted the backboards up, fastening them flush with the wall. It was another few days before the hoops went up. But when they did, even without nets, I started firing away.

I was all over that gym floor, racing around, madly dribbling, jumping, chasing the ball, trying not to look at it, having it bounce off my feet in every direction. But I was also shooting. I had no form, knew nothing, couldn't seem to imitate others I had seen, so I just kept winging it up there.

The only shots that dropped through were due to the law of averages, but for some reason I wasn't discouraged. I knew there was no way a twelve-year-old would ever make the Globetrotters without learning to shoot, and so I knew I would learn. I wasn't sure how.

My dribbling and ballhandling were awkward and primitive, and I was shooting probably less than 10 percent successfully. No doubt any defender could have blocked or stolen my shots. But one day my break came, just like I knew it would.

I had decided to stand under the basket and keep shooting until something dropped in twice in a row. Twenty minutes later, I was still trying. Pushing, jumping, flinging, arching. No matter what I tried, I couldn't buy two baskets in a row. One would swish. Twelve shots later, one would bank in off the backboard. I sensed someone watching me.

I was a little self-conscious, being so thin and such a poor shooter. I stole a glance behind me. Sure enough, Earl Jackson was watching me. He was a stocky, muscular man who had been a star high-school athlete and had gone to North Carolina State on a football scholarship. A knee injury sent him back home after the first year, and now he was helping out in the Boys' Club.

At North Carolina State, a basketball player named Henry Thomas (a junior star out of Pennsylvania who was nicknamed

Big Dog) took a liking to Earl and taught him to play basketball with both hands. Earl edged over to me as I tried harder and harder to make the ball go through the hoop. That rim seemed twenty feet over my head.

"Hey, Slim. C'mere and let me show you somethin'." He didn't wait for an answer, and he didn't think it unusual to teach a beginner an unusual shot. He could see I didn't even know how to hold the ball, and it was clear I had weak wrists and ankles, but he had also seen me working at it alone every day.

Earl positioned me carefully, showed me how to cradle the ball in one hand, protect it from a defender, move away from the basket, pivot, reach high over my shoulder and head for a hook shot, and let it fly.

There was so much to remember, and I was embarrassed when I forgot a step or a turn or the ball went straight up or straight down. Earl didn't wait until I made one. He just showed me how to do it and told me to practice it for a while. That was a mistake. A mistake that started a career. Earl forgot about me for several weeks.

He was busy helping with the new club. There was organizing to do, other kids to help, games to referee, his own workouts to fit in. I didn't know what to do except to keep practicing the only shot I had been taught. It felt awkward. I felt ridiculous. But I had seen Earl make that shot. And he told me to practice it.

I shot and shot and shot and shot. A couple of times the ball dropped through the net, but somehow I knew it wasn't because I had done anything right. Maybe I had stepped wrong, pivoted too far, launched it too low. I didn't know. All I knew was that it didn't feel right, even if it had gone through.

One day it all came together. I had been visualizing the shot during the day, before I got to the gym. I had been trying to get comfortable with it in my mind. I eagerly grabbed the ball and ran to the hoop. I was loose. I dribbled around a little. I stepped into position and walked through the steps of the right-hand hook shot. It felt right. I dribbled, drew the ball into position, pivoted, shot, and missed.

But it had felt right! Not awkward, not ridiculous. The shot had just missed, like lots of shots just missed. It wasn't because of bad form or anything. I had the technique down. I shot again. The ball bounced on the rim, hit the backboard, and dropped through. A little sloppy, but I didn't care. I had a shot, and it felt right.

I shot again. The ball was long and bounced off the side of the rim. But again, it had felt right. I had missed by less than an inch. It was dead on but a little strong. I shot again and took a little off. Time stood still. I could feel this shot from my toes through my finger tips. The mechanics had become ingrained. I could concentrate on the one aspect of the shot that would make it or break it, the launch itself.

I willed that ball right through the hoop. It touched nothing but net, and I saw it all the way. It felt perfect. I raced after the ball and hurried back into position. A dribble, the maneuver, the shot, right on but a little strong. Too excited. Try again. Right on but a little short. Overcompensated. Try again. Swish Again. Swish. Again. Swish.

I hardly knew how to handle the ball. I had never played except with a milk can or a tennis ball on a wire rim in a tree. But I had a shot. I kept firing until I could hardly get my hands over my head. I could make that shot more than half the time. It was from only one spot on the floor, and I walked through it the same way every time, but that hoop was no longer the enemy.

I was connected to it. I felt it was part of me. I had control of the ball and its curve, and I could will that ball through the hoop. Sweet Georgia Brown, I was getting somewhere!

4

The Spark of Stick-to-itiveness

I was awkward, gangly, going through puberty, and I ached all over, all the time. My friends complained of the same things. We decided it was just because we were growing so fast.

I wanted to learn the game of basketball so bad that it broke my heart to see how many of the other kids seemed to take to it naturally. There were pickup games at either end of the gym all the time, but I knew I couldn't compete with the older guys at all. I just stood at a free basket and kept shooting my hook shot. It was all I knew.

Finally, Earl Jackson noticed me again. I had been watching him and waiting for weeks, but I was too shy to ask for any more help. He didn't have to say anything. He just came over and watched me for a few minutes. I was really nervous, but I pulled myself together to show him that I had mastered the shot the best I could.

He moved left of the basket and signaled me to follow. "Here's how you do it with the other hand, Slim. It'll feel a little awkward at first." Earl walked through it twice, swishing both shots. He made it look so easy. Could it really be any more difficult than from the right side? Surely it couldn't feel more awkward than the first time from the right.

It was. Mercifully, Earl walked away after flipping me the ball. I went a half-hour before I even hit the backboard, and then the ball bounced off it and went onto center court where the older guys were playing. They swore at me as I sheepishly retrieved the ball. I waited until the attention was off me before trying the left-handed hook shot again.

Eventually, of course, the shot came around, just as Earl knew it would. He told me later that he saw something in me, some tenacity, some spirit that would keep me on that court, working day after day. I told myself that I wouldn't shoot my right-hand shot until I made three left-handers in a row. That meant very little right-hand shooting for a while, but soon enough, sooner than the right-hander had felt comfortable, I had developed both shots.

It was fun, and I kept at it. I was still weak but felt myself building up some. Mr. Walter Bess, who ran the club, had his athletic director, E. L. Haynes, toss a medicine ball (a ten-pound ball used to strengthen the hands and wrists) back and forth with me, but it was several days before I could handle the heavy ball without dropping it every other time.

I couldn't see the value in catching a ball that nearly knocked me over each time, and I could hardly find the power to toss it back farther than five or six feet. Then I went back to the basketball and realized it felt like a feather. That wasn't the purpose of the medicine ball, Mr. Bess told me. It was to build strength. But making the normal basketball feel lighter was a definite benefit.

I grew to admire Earl and Mr. Haynes and Mr. Bess. They did everything they had to do to keep the club open. Funds were scarce, and the fifty-cents-a-year dues were hardly paid by anyone, certainly not me. We all knew Mr. Bess was carrying much of the financial load himself, just because he believed in the program and loved the kids.

His wife, Ruby Bess, was my seventh-grade teacher, and she got me to quit slouching when I walked down the hall. I was getting close to five nine or five ten by then, making me tower over my classmates. Mrs. Bess would point at me and say, "Meadow! Meadow Lemon! You stand up, boy. You're not going to be runty like these little people. Stand up straight and tall."

She always made me feel special because she admired my cartooning and drawing. She made me think that if anything happened to my goal of becoming a Harlem Globetrotter, I could always become an artist. I still like to think I could have.

I hadn't told too many people about my dream yet, because so many of them were better players than I was. Those who did know ridiculed me. I didn't need that, but I didn't care. All I needed was determination to become a Trotter, and I had enough of that for a whole team.

When I dreamed and fantasized about playing with the Globetrotters, I never saw myself in the starring role as clown prince. I just wanted to be a team member, to be part of it, to contribute to making people laugh and clap and enjoy. I wanted that feeling of family and teamwork that I never really had. I'd never seen a Globetrotter in person, yet something drew me to them as if they would finally be my first real home and family.

Sometime during this period I handwrote "Goose" on the side of the little canvas duffel bag I carried to school and to the club. People started calling me Goose, and most of them knew he was my idol. Some teased me, but I didn't care anymore.

One day I was walking to the club, and I overheard Joe Maguire, owner of a local candy shop, ask his friend, "Where does that little black boy think he's goin' every day? He's never gonna amount to nothin'."

That made my ears burn, but it also made me even more determined. Joe Maguire was as black as I was, and he eventually became another helper at the Boys' Club. He was to see me grow as a player and indeed "amount to" something. When I had been with the Globetrotters four or five years, I sent him an eight-by-ten glossy of me in uniform and signed it "To my friend Joe Maguire. Just look at me now. Meadowlark Lemon." We still laugh with each other about how important he was in motivating me.

Wallace Keils and I decided to go out for the varsity football team the year that I was in seventh grade and he was in sixth. We were both tall for our ages, and we didn't know you had to be in high school to play on the team. We both went out for receiver, and Wallace also punted.

We showed up in the locker room, got suited up, and had our names written on a clipboard. Wallace punted twenty yards farther than the varsity punter, and I was making one-handed catches over some defenders who had played on the school's championship team the year before.

It was clear the coaches were taking notice. I saw them watching us and making notes on the clipboard. But then they asked us the names of our homeroom teachers. We told them.

"There's no teachers at Williston High with those names, boys."

"We're in the junior high."

They laughed and laughed. "Come back when you're in high school."

We took those words as encouragement. The fall that I went into the eighth grade I started to hang around the high school, and I got to know the varsity basketball coach, Frank Robinson. Unfortunately, I didn't make much of an impression on him. To him I was just another skinny kid who didn't look much like an athlete. I knew I could play football and was a good defensive baseball player, but basketball was going to be my game. I asked him if there was an old ball around I could have. The Boys' Club wasn't open all the time, and I wanted a ball I could take with me.

The only thing he came up with was an old leather basketball with a gaping tear in one side. There would be no repairing or replacing the bladder. That ball was beyond ever inflating again, but I was grateful to have anything. I hurried home, and during the time I should have been working out at the Boys' Club, I carefully stuffed that old ball with paper, comic books, and rags until it filled out and looked normal.

I was proud of myself and excited. I knew it wouldn't bounce, of course, but it was the right size and shape and would give me the feel of a real basketball. Then I held it for the first time. It weighed closer to the medicine ball than a basketball.

Still, I had my own ball. The Boys' Club would be closing for the evening, so I charged across the street and tried a few hook shots at my coat-hanger/onion-sack basketball net. The first several didn't get far over my head, but finally, I hit one. The rim, the net, the nails, everything but the tree came down with the ball. Later that night I sneaked out and went into the white school playground, where they had finally put up outdoor metal backboards and rims. The nets had long since been torn away.

I rounded up a few friends, some who used to think basketball was a sissy game, and we began sneaking into that school yard every night to shoot some hoops. I had to listen for my dad coming home from work or from gambling someplace, but at least we weren't noisy enough playing basketball to draw the police.

It was so dark that two guys had to stand under the rim to tell whether our shots went in. The only ball we had was mine with the stuffing in it, so mostly we just passed and shot in the dark. I suppose it shouldn't be any wonder that several of us went on to be outstanding ballplayers at various levels of the game.

In the afternoons I went to the Boys' Club and watched the pickup games and tried to get in a few. It bothered me that I wasn't able to get the rhythm of the game. Some of the guys were naturals. Thusalem floated around the court with a sense of where everyone was. He could play defense, dribble, pass, and shoot. It seemed everyone was better than I was.

When I got into a little game and the ball came to me, I panicked. I wound up throwing it out of bounds or freezing and having someone tie me up for a jump ball. Then my timing was so bad I couldn't outjump even guys who were shorter.

I was running with Willie Dixon then, the guy we called Bunny. He was a soft-spoken, low-voiced guy that everyone liked. He was a pretty good athlete, too. Ed Sutton and Bunny and I spent a lot of time at the club, but when I hung with Edward Martin, I seemed to get into trouble.

Edward Martin was the kind of guy who liked to be in control. He was older than we were and had really been around. If everybody else was doing one thing, he wanted to do another. He didn't want anyone telling him what to do, not Earl, not E. L. Haynes, not even Mr. Bess. Every time he went to the Boys' Club he wound up getting run off by one of the leaders. And usually, I followed him out.

Earl started lecturing me about that one day. "Let me tell you somethin', Slim. You're not a bad guy. You don't give nobody no trouble. How you gonna learn this game if you keep hangin' with him? You come in here with him, and you don't do nothin'. And every time he say, 'Let's go,' you go. You got to take a stand one of these days, Slim, and live your own life." Earl turned his back on me and hopped up on a little stage where the boxing ring was located.

Edward Martin, who was a much better athlete than I was, had already gotten Mr. Haynes mad at him. Now he was horsing around with someone else. Soon he was bored. "Let's go, Meadow."

I didn't say anything. I looked up at Earl. His back was still turned, but I knew he had heard Edward and was listening for my response.

"C'mon, Lemon! Let's go!"

Earl started to turn and look.

I spoke quietly, "No. I'm staying."

Ever since that day, I've made my own decisions. I've made some bad ones. Some heartbreaking ones. But they have been mine, and I can live with the consequences. I stayed in that gym and tried to get into every game I could. Earl and Mr. Haynes and Mr. Bess gave their time to all of us, walking us through the fundamentals, teaching us, inspiring us, making us work at it.

My goal seemed dimmer because I was uncoordinated and everyone else was so good at the game, but still there was nothing I'd rather be than a Globetrotter. I tried to believe Earl when he said I would eventually get used to my growing body. He told me that even if I didn't make it, I might be a doctor or a lawyer or a real estate agent when I grew up. But he never told me I could never be a professional basketball player. He thought it more than once, he tells me now, but he didn't want to discourage me. There was just enough spark of stick-to-itiveness there that he wouldn't rule out anything.

It got to where I was looking to get into a basketball game anywhere I could find one. The R. R. Taylor Homes was a housing project with a gymnasium where lots of good players worked out. I spent a lot of time there, and I began to feel a little more comfortable on the court. I wasn't anywhere near the best, of course, but at least I could slow down and think when I had the ball; I could find the open man, maybe get a rebound or two once in a while.

I rarely shot, let alone sank one, but when I did, it was usually a hook and drew lots of catcalls. I wasn't being stupid or playing hot dog. It was the only shot I really knew. But I started learning a few more by watching and listening. And by taking the advice so freely offered at the Boys' Club.

One night Chester Green and I were in a pickup game at the Taylor Projects. I was playing on the skins team. The ball rolled to me, and I found myself tearing down the court for a lay-up with no one near me. I had practiced making the shot and then pushing off the wall with my foot to head back down the court at top speed.

The shot wasn't pretty, but it rolled in. I pushed off the wall and expected a little reaction from both teams for having made it, but as I charged up court, no one was even watching. They were staring at two young guys who had come in with shotguns. I screeched to a halt and froze, just as one of them fired toward the ceiling.

Someone shut off the lights, and that place emptied in two seconds. I raced for the nearest exit, my shirt still wadded in a corner somewhere. I tore down the street as fast as my legs could carry me as more shotgun blasts rang out.

I never learned what the trouble was, and I never retrieved my shirt either. But I did learn something. Chester Green was a boy with average to below-average speed. That night he flew by me so fast I thought I was standing still. Adrenaline can do wonderful things to your abilities.

Not long after that, I was working on my game at the Boys' Club when who should walk in unannounced but Titty Boo himself. He was alone this time, and even though it had been more than two years since he'd beaten me up, the emotion surged back instantly. I didn't even have time to be scared.

In fact, I felt better enough about myself that I didn't even hesitate. I had worked out in the boxing ring at the club, and that gave me the confidence to charge him. Right then and there. Before he even knew who or what hit him, I was all over him. I bumped him, pushed him, and started swinging at him. He hardly had time to react. "Who's this? What's your problem?"

"You remember me, Titty Boo!"

Mr. Haynes jumped between us. "You boys want to settle somethin' with your fists, you get into the ring or get outta here, you hear?"

I was ready. "In the ring! You ready, Boo?"

"Wha'd I ever do to you?"

"Don't play dumb! You chicken?"

We stepped into the ring with gloves on and a crowd to watch. Titty Boo was still off guard. I knew he remembered why I wanted a piece of him, but my eagerness was intimidating him. He tried to look tough and mean, and he was still bigger than I was, though no longer that much taller.

When Mr. Haynes signaled us to fight, I drilled old Titty Boo. I mean, I hit him ten times for every time he even tried to swing at me. To the stomach, to the jaw, to the head, to the ear, I was beatin' on him. He was huffing and puffing and wobbling, trying to hold on. I was running through my mind the last time we had "fought." I was being held by his friends while he punched *and* kicked me.

I wouldn't let up, even when he tumbled to one knee and covered his head with his gloves. Mr. Haynes needed Earl's help to pull me off him. I'm glad they did. I might still be punching him.

My dad had told me, "Never let anyone get the better of you." He said there's always someone who wants to run your life. "You got to establish yourself early, boy. Then they'll leave you alone."

I still had a score to settle with Red Sumpter. He beat me up or took my money every time he saw me at the movies. He was a good basketball player and was at the club quite often, but I avoided him. I got a sinking feeling in the pit of my stomach whenever I even thought of him, but my revenge against Titty Boo gave me more confidence.

The next Saturday, standing in line with my friends at the Ritz, I was determined to fight back if ol' Red Sumpter tried anything. I kept telling myself that I was a man, not a mouse, and that I would never forgive myself if I gave in and let him take my money again.

When he showed up, swaggering toward us with his hand out like he was making his regular collection, I exploded. I hauled off and hit that boy so hard I just dropped him to the sidewalk. Then I took off running like I have never run before, except maybe that night at the Taylor Projects.

The next Monday at school, Geney Boy, an instigator, was there doin' his thing. He wanted to see a fight, so he kept chirping away about how he just knew Red wasn't going to let this pass.

Red might have, but not after that. The story got around how I had flattened him at the Ritz, so I had to face the music. He beat me so bad, I can still taste the dirt. He knocked me down, rolled on top of me, and smashed my head and face into the ground. I wound up with dirt in my hair, eyes, and mouth.

Red knew he had my number after that, so he treated me like dirt during Boys' Club tryouts and in pickup games, but finally I had had enough. I might get beat up again, but I wasn't going to take any more of that. The guys would think I was a coward.

Red started hassling me, and I attacked him. For some reason, none of the adults broke it up or insisted we get in the ring. Maybe they knew it just had to be this way. If I was ever going to play on the Boys' Club team, I was going to have to have some sort of an understanding with Red Sumpter.

We rassled all over the floor for several minutes with neither of us taking or giving too much. Finally, it ended. It was just over. Neither won or lost. Red stuck his hand out. I shook it. "Guess I'd better quit tryin' to push you around, Goose."

I nodded, and we played a lot of ball together after that—as friends, not enemies.

5

Number 13

With all the characters I had been afraid of either settled up with or turned into friends, I could concentrate on basketball. Worrying whether you're going to meet up with someone is a distraction that doesn't contribute to making you a good athlete in any sport.

It wasn't that I was looking for a fight or wanted to be king of the hill. I had finally learned that someone will always be there to test you, and if you want to put that behind you and get on with business, you've got to be prepared to put up or shut up.

I was still skinny and awkward, but I soon developed a reputation as an okay guy with a good sense of humor, a versatile athlete, and someone who wasn't easily pushed around. That was just what I wanted. I was deficient in the girlfriend department (I didn't have *any*), especially compared to some of my friends, but from watching the high schoolers, I knew that would change if I became a varsity athlete.

The best preparation I could think of for high-school basketball was the Boys' Club team. They had openings for thirteen players. When I looked around at my buddies and all the guys from the Taylor Homes, I figured I was about fifteenth in ability. I was, however, first in dedication and hard work.

My dad and the men at the Boys' Club had been preaching for years that those were the kinds of qualities that paid off, but I didn't want to be thought of only as a kid who showed a lot of spunk. They were going to suit up their best thirteen ballplayers, and the rest would just have to wait.

Until the tryouts, I made it a point to spend every spare minute down at the club. That winter I hurried home from eighth grade every day, dropped off my books, and sprinted to the club to play basketball until dinner time. On Saturdays I was there all day. We always started by choosing up sides for a pickup game, which included Mr. Haynes, Earl Jackson, and several other adults. I was usually picked among the last, but at least I was getting to play.

Maybe nobody else noticed, but I had pretty well mastered the hook shot with either hand and from virtually anywhere within fifteen feet of the basket. Because the other guys were more naturally talented, I found myself having to go to the hook more often and having to shoot it from farther out. I thought it was dropping in fairly consistently—in fact, I knew it was. But it was such an unorthodox shot that everyone always howled when it went in, as if it was luck. Until I started making it more than half the time, it remained a secret weapon because no one worried about it.

I was thin and light enough to get pushed away from the bucket and outpositioned most of the time, so that long hook became my best weapon. Though I had improved on defense and had become a fairly good passer, most everyone knew who was going to make that basketball team. I doubt they thought of me.

Red Sumpter would be a starter, of course, along with Earl Goss, Geney Boy, Spook, Pipe (who was even skinnier than I was), and Earl (Sonny Boy) Jacobs. Sonny Boy was probably the best player from the Taylor Projects, and I'd had him score over, under, around, and through me enough times to convince me.

But who would make up the seven reserves? I wanted it so bad I could taste it. Rumors said the team would play some of the smaller area high schools. Genuine competition. We'd find out what we were made of. I worked harder than ever.

Then came the day, not long before the tryouts, when I pulled a stunt that could have cost me any hope of making the team. I was playing in a pickup game and was guarded by Mr. Haynes. He was a big man, about six two and 240 pounds. He moved real well and had to hold himself back from dominating the younger players.

He guarded me close, and I wanted to impress him, even if this wasn't the actual tryout. I considered any chance to play against the adults or the better players an opportunity to show I was worthy of the team.

I spun away from him and dribbled toward the baseline where I planned to launch a fifteen- to eighteen-foot hook shot. I hadn't yet learned to keep my nonshooting arm up to protect the ball, and Mr. Haynes sliced a hand in to slap the ball away. I tightened my grip at the last instant, and the ball dropped and hit me on the thigh, then his knee, and went out of bounds.

To me, it was clearly off him last and should be our ball. He saw otherwise. "Out off you! Our ball!"

I exploded. "No! It hit you last!"

He ignored me with a tolerant smile. "Our ball. C'mon, let's go." He grabbed it and held it over his head, expecting me to defend against the inbounds pass. But I wasn't going to take it just because he was an adult. He was wrong, and it wasn't fair.

I stormed off the court. "I'm never coming back here to play again!"

Earl Jackson ran to catch up with me at the door. He put a hand on each of my shoulders. "Listen to me, Slim, you don't want to do this."

"Yes, I do! Leave me alone!"

"Listen, boy, if you don't play here, where you gonna play? You know well as I do you ain't got nowhere else to play. You got to play here."

He was getting through, but pride and anger gripped me. "I don't care. I won't play at all then."

I remember his next words as if he said them yesterday. His voice was soft, but earnest. "Slim, sometimes you got to kiss butt before you can kick butt, you understand?"

I did, but I wasn't in the mood to nod. I shrugged and turned away. But I didn't leave. I went back and hung around the game until they worked me back in, and to Mr. Haynes's credit, he acted as if nothing had happened. When I had time to think about it, I knew he wasn't the type who would make a bad call on purpose. He called it the way he saw it.

Tryouts came, and I was hopeful. I did the best I knew how in all the drills. I heard some of the guys say that the coaches always looked for defense and passing skills, and though my shooting and ballhandling weren't the best yet, I could defend and pass. In defense, I got in everybody's face. I imagined trying to get into their shoes, into their uniforms with them. I was going to be an irritant, in their way, on their case. They would see more of me than the ball.

I wanted to keep guys from getting any passes at all. If they got a pass, I didn't want them to dribble without dribbling right on my toes. And if they dribbled, I didn't want them to get off a shot. If they got off a shot, I didn't want it to be a good one. If it was a good one, I wanted to outposition them for the rebound.

Somehow, miraculously, when the list of thirteen was posted, my name was right at the bottom, number thirteen. I was thrilled to get a jersey, to get to sit on a bench, to maybe play a few minutes at the end of each game. Best of all, I got to practice against the starters every day.

The coaches at the Boys' Club gave the team members the most attention when it came to teaching fundamentals. When I remember their patience, especially with me, it makes me want to be a better coach to young professionals. They demonstrated things to us. They walked us through every shot, every pass, every defense, every play.

We got plays wrong ten or eleven times in a row, yet they found the good points, then walked us through it again. During the season, I memorized everything I had been taught. I don't apologize for saying I worked harder than anyone. I had to.

I was there early and left late, always working on some aspect of my game. There were other sports I wanted to play, especially football, but my sights were still set on making the Harlem Globetrotters, so basketball would always be top priority.

Eventually, my game improved to the point where I wasn't just one of the scrubs that finished the lost causes or the blowouts. The team was winning about half its games and staying fairly competitive even in most of the losses, so I was also learning a lot about strategy.

I worked my way up to the top ten and was called on in special situations where a rested ballhandler or defensive specialist was needed. I was putting through a few shots other than my patented hooks, and soon I was the second or third sub to go into a game.

By the end of the basketball season, I was playing almost two quarters a game and was truly affecting the outcome. I had a long, long way to go and was nowhere near ready to compete on any other level, but I was getting a glimpse of what it was all about. I loved it.

What I hoped for was that day when the entire game would seem natural to me, when I could glide up and down the court, accelerating, decelerating, pivoting, moving, passing, shooting with confidence and with a sense that my body was made for that. I was nearly five eleven and growing, and I felt stronger all the time. What I wanted was court presence, total command of my physical skills. I had good hands and quickness, and I thought I knew the game. My goal was to break into that starting line-up the next year. I would be a freshman at Williston Industrial High School, but I couldn't hope to play there my first year. They had a super team coming back from a good year.

During that summer, just before starting high school, I started to feel more comfortable with my body. I jogged onto the court, dribbling, loosening up, and I didn't feel as if my arms and legs were going four different directions. I could control the ball. My hands were big, and I could almost palm the ball. My timing was good, so I was already able to slam dunk, though that was considered the lowest form of street basketball.

My friends and I had some wild times just goofing around. It was almost as if we knew our childhood days were coming to a close and we had to get some craziness out of our systems. Somewhere we got hold of an old, beat-up car for about twenty-five dollars, and a bunch of us thought it would be a good idea to drive it down to Sea Breeze, the "blacks-only beach," and show off a little. You couldn't find Sea Breeze on many maps, but it was near Carolina Beach. Somebody either got beat up, cut up, shot up, or killed there every weekend.

Jimmy Lofton was the only one of us who could drive, and every time he started the thing up, it overheated and started billowing steam. We took several gallons of water with us and piled in—Bunny, Chester, Bap, and all the rest.

We had to stop every couple of miles to let the radiator chug-alug another gallon of water. Once, when Jimmy started it back up, it wouldn't go but one direction: in reverse. He swung it around and backed his way toward Sea Breeze with the rest of us howling till we cried.

By the time we got to the beach, we were almost out of water, so we delayed filling the radiator until we couldn't see for the steam. Everyone could see us, though. We got quite the reaction on the beach. We heard the cops were looking for us, probably wondering if we had a title or license. Of course we had neither.

We decided to get out of there at dusk. We filled up the gallon jugs, and Jimmy backed us all the way into Brooklyn. From a distance we could see a squad car, but we didn't know if it was after us or not. We told Jimmy. He sped up. The steam billowed.

One of us (guess who?) crawled out onto the hood to fill the radiator—in flight. Jimmy was steering by looking through the back window anyway, and we couldn't afford to stop. By then, Jimmy had that thing floored, and the water wasn't making much of an impact on the radiator. Besides the steam, black smoke belched from somewhere underneath. We weren't going to make it back to the neighborhood, and the cops were gaining on us.

When the squad car's red lights flashed, we knew they were after us. It was all Jimmy could do to keep the thing going straight, and we must have been pushing twenty-five miles an hour in reverse. Somebody noticed we were coming up on the cemetery, and we all started shouting, "Pull in here! We'll ditch it!"

That car was nearly on fire by the time Jimmy hit the brakes, and we rolled between a couple of headstones. It was hot and smoking, but we didn't hang around to watch. We all took off in different directions, hurdling graves and the fence. We were long gone by the time the cops pulled in.

Shoot, we'd hoped to sell that thing and get at least half the original investment out of it.

6

The Big Break

Williston Industrial, the only black high school in Wilmington, had about four hundred students. I was apprehensive the first day, just like all the other freshmen. I ran around mostly with Son Gillyard, Edward and Alfred Martin, Ed Sutton, Bunny Dixon, Chester Green, and Bap Boyd.

Son was crazy as ever. We had one teacher who was so pretty, Son kept bragging about how he was going to get next to her. She had a habit of sitting on students' desks as she roamed around the room.

Son said next time she sat on his desk, he was going to put his hand out so she'd sit on it. We laughed. "Man, you'll never do that! Huh-uh, you never would!"

One day as she was talking, she absent-mindedly strolled near Son's desk. Several of us poked each other and pointed, trying to keep from giggling. Sure enough, ol' Son laid his hand right there flat on the desk, and she sat square on it. You should have seen the looks on both their faces!

She jumped up, took one step, and slapped Son so hard across the face that tears just started streamin' down. "Don't you ever do that again, Richard Gillyard! You hear me?"

He was as mad as she was and just as embarrassed. He yelled over his shoulder as he ran from the room, "I'm goin' home and tell my sister Arlene, and she's goin' to come here and beat you up!" He told us he would have told his mother if she wasn't so old. He didn't come back to school for three days, and the thing blew over.

Chester Green was probably the best-looking kid in our group, and he bragged all the time about how smooth he was going to be with the girls at the next party. There was one girl who was real sweet on him, but when it came time to prove his words, he ran. He was just too shy. He used to eat his lunch in the bathroom to stay away from the girls.

I reminded him of that when I visited Wilmington recently, and he denied it up and down. He says I mooched food off the girls later in high school, but I don't remember that. I do remember Chester carrying his books in a couple of old saddle bags that he tied together with a string and slung around his neck. We started calling him Horse.

The first thing I wanted to do at Williston was to go out for football. From playing in the neighborhood all my life, I'd developed a love for blocking and tackling and a talent for catching passes with one hand.

One of the most interesting people I met on the football field was a player named Robert Brooks. We called him Iron Man because he had a naturally muscular body, and when he sweated, his bulging muscles looked like chunks of iron. He was probably the most gifted all-around athlete I've ever seen.

He could play every position in football, basketball, and baseball and was better at each one than anyone else on the team. He was a strange bird, though. He hated school and only showed up when he had to take a test. I guess he thought high school was like college. They let him get away with it for the sake of the athletic teams, I suppose, and because he was a brilliant student.

Our science teacher, Mrs. Lofton, would sit him in a corner and give him a customized test, much tougher than the one the rest of us took. She probably thought that if he was going to get away with just waltzing in on test day, he was going to have to prove himself. Within fifteen or twenty minutes, he'd saunter up to her desk with a smirk, drop off the test, and leave. Mrs. Lofton would grade the test and shake her head. "He did it again."

That first year of high school was also when I met one of the most influential men in my life, E. A. (Spike) Corbin. He was assistant football and basketball coach and head baseball coach. He seemed to like me right off because I enjoyed hitting and wasn't afraid to work hard. He had a home twenty miles outside Wilmington, and I started going out there with Earl Jackson and a few other people to just talk or shoot hoops. Coach Corbin says that I adopted him, and I guess in a way I did. He became like a second father to me.

I was learning masonry at school, and Coach Corbin let me tear down his brick barbecue pit and rebuild it with him. Earl used to bring along a guy who could really cook, and we'd enjoy feasts out there before and after our private basketball workouts.

I was young and not very big for a varsity football player, and I hadn't developed much speed yet. I won a starting role on defense, but other teams quickly caught on to the fact that I was a freshman and started attacking my zone, usually successfully.

Before our league season began, we played a couple of schools from South Carolina, one from Columbia and one from Charleston. In Charleston I had to guard a senior running back with a reputation. His name was J. C. Caroline, who wound up playing for many years in the National Football League. What a way to start a season!

He tore me up. I was left watching him most of the game as he caught everything thrown his way. I took a lot of good-natured ribbing from my teammates, but my performance ate away at me. I asked for a tackling dummy to practice on at home, and Coach Corbin talked the head coach, Coach Robinson, into letting me have one. I practiced constantly.

The next three years I started on offense and defense and was named all-state all three seasons.

Off the athletic field, I was shy. Coach Robinson's wife taught speech and kept trying to talk me into taking her class. I couldn't think of anything more terrifying, and I never took it. She also encouraged me to take a foreign language, but I couldn't imagine ever needing one. Now that I've played on every continent and have my own television talk show, I can see why I should have taken both those courses.

One of my teachers, Mrs. Leonard, used to tell troublemakers or goof-offs, "I will see you in Philippi!" I wondered for years what that meant until I visited Wilmington last year and another of my teachers told me that Philippi was the site of a Roman war during the reign of Julius Caesar. You learn something new every day.

Coach Corbin was one of the busiest teachers at Williston. He taught six classes a day in physical education or health and hygiene, plus he had a homeroom and sponsored the drama club. Coaching was on top of all that.

He was a little intense on the health courses. A lot of the coaches went pretty easy in that and let the athletes get away with murder. Not Coach Corbin. In his mind, it was just as important to get a good education as it was to become a great athlete. I learned the entire anatomical system in that health class of his.

Coach Corbin became head coach of the major sports long after I left school, and eventually he was named director of athletics for all the Wilmington high schools, quite a prestigious position. I don't know what kind of a salary level he reached when he finally retired several years ago, but when he was coaching me, he was making eighteen cents an hour. Fact.

Just before the basketball season, Coach Corbin had us playing basketball in gym class. He liked the way I moved. "You're going out for basketball, aren't you, Meadows?" (He still calls me Meadows.)

"I play at the Boys' Club."

"With Earl, I know, but I think you could help us. We're going to need a center."

I was stunned. Frankly, I knew better. There was a guy on the football team named Willie (Jukie) Johnson who was about six three and 225, and he looked like a world beater. He was center in the varsity basketball team, and I hadn't even been a starter for the Boys' Club yet. Coach Corbin encouraged me to talk to Coach Robinson, who was also head basketball coach. "Tell him you want a shot."

I didn't have the courage to say that. I did tell Coach Robinson that Coach Corbin had asked me to introduce myself to him and that I would like to play basketball for him. He was cordial and friendly, but he didn't even invite me to try out. He didn't see anything in me, and apparently at that point, he thought Jukie was his answer at center.

Coach Corbin confided in me later that he thought Jukie was a good football player but he wasn't aggressive enough on the basketball court. He had physical attributes, but he couldn't jump. I hardly knew the game, yet Coach Corbin recognized my potential.

Coach Corbin told Coach Robinson, "You're missing the bet with Johnson in there when Lemon is available. This is a kid who could play center for us standing on his head."

Robinson disagreed. He said, "Johnson can do the job. Don't bother with Lemon for now."

I wasn't hurt or disappointed. I not only hadn't been looking for a spot on the high-school team but honestly didn't believe I was ready. To me, the Boys' Club team was good training, and I had a lot to learn. Let's face it. I hadn't really faced any of the competition that a big school like Williston faces.

I found, however, that when I went out for the Boys' Club team again, something was different. Knowing of Coach Corbin's confidence in me, I played with more intensity, more aggressiveness, more sense of purpose. I had the feeling that when my game came together, I would get my opportunities. My goal now was to make the starting five. The previous year I had moved up from thirteenth to about eighth, and a couple of guys were now too old to play on the team.

That put me sixth with the returning players, but there were newcomers trying out, too. I couldn't coast. Now was the time to turn a corner. I was filling out, but not much. I was stronger than I'd ever been, and I was developing speed and quickness. The football season must have provided some of that. I also enjoyed playing a sport where you didn't wake up every morning feeling like you'd had your head kicked in.

Whatever it was, my game, at least on the local neighborhood level, had come together. Almost immediately I was one of the top two players on the Boys' Club team. Though I was still young, I was a leader in passing, dribbling, ballhandling, defense, rebounding, and shooting.

My one-handed hook shot surprised people—myself included—because I seemed to get so high off the ground. I didn't plan it, hadn't worked on that aspect of it, but with football and physical maturing, my legs were stronger. When I went up for a shot, I rose far above everyone else, and that, of course, made it easier to shoot successfully.

Earl also felt that I followed my shots well, outpositioning most and getting a lot of rebounds. When the season started, I was the first-string center. I played with a vengeance. I was getting superb grounding in fundamentals from Earl and Mr. Haynes, and I loved the game.

When I wanted a real lesson in how the game was to be played, I watched the Williston varsity. They were something. Coach Corbin had been right about Jukie Johnson. He was a little slow in the middle, but he held his own under the boards and fed the good shooters. Williston started to win from the opening game, and they just kept winning.

It seemed a whole different brand of basketball. I knew where I was competing was good for me, but compared to the high-school games, we were in slow motion. To see Williston Industrial streaking up and down the court, dominating their opponents with some of my older friends right in the thick of it, man, that was basketball. I wondered if I'd ever be ready.

Just past midway through the high-school season, Williston had won its first sixteen games and was ranked first in the state, even ahead of the school where Sam Jones played center. Jones, then a junior, went on to become a star for the Boston Celtics for many years.

The games, however, were getting tougher. Everyone was out to get them, and Jukie Johnson wasn't able to compete with the real topnotch centers around the state. Eventually, probably trying to play above his level of capability, he was injured. The high-school team staggered through the next couple of games with a reserve center, but they would play against Sam Jones soon, and things looked dim.

Coach Corbin scouted a couple of the Boys' Club's games. Then he brought Coach Robinson with him. I didn't think anything about why they might be there until they approached me after a game. Coach Robinson was a pleasant, dignified man. He said, "Meadow, Coach Corbin has told me a lot about you. Says you play some defense and that you really get up there on that push shot. I can see that you do. You know, a lot of my current team is going to graduate after this season, and I need to start building for next year. What would you think about suiting up for us and learning the ropes for the remainder of this year? Then you'll be ready maybe to play regularly for us next year."

I was speechless. He couldn't be serious.

7

Welcome to the Real Thing

Even though a decision to join the high-school team meant I couldn't play for the Boys' Club, Earl couldn't have been more encouraging. He insisted that it was a good break for me and that I should jump at it. "That team could wind up undefeated, Slim. They've won every game they've played so far. Twenty-eight games! They're the best team around."

"But I'm not sure I'm ready."

"How you ever gonna know? They ain't askin' you to carry the team. You're just gonna get a little taste of what it's all about so you can help 'em when all those seniors graduate."

I really didn't feel ready, but I wasn't going to pass up that opportunity for anything. I'll never forget working out with the varsity. They reacted coolly to me at first, of course, the way any team does to the new guy who hasn't proved himself yet. The problem was, I wasn't ready to prove myself for quite a while. When they ran through their regular drills, I was concentrating so hard on where to go and what to do with the ball, I dropped passes, took shots I shouldn't have, and basically looked like the raw freshman I was.

The coaches, however, were patient. They saw something in me that I hoped was there, that I wanted to be there, but that I didn't see in myself yet. I was just barely six feet tall, but that level of competition made me feel weak, slow, awkward, and small. Though this was a topnotch team, it was a small team, and even then six of the players were taller than I was.

What a feeling to pull on that colorful uniform the first time! We jogged out for our warm-up in front of a capacity home crowd, and I was proud. I wouldn't start. I probably wouldn't sub, even if we were up by 30 with a minute to go. But I was a member of the team. I had that uniform. I had learned the warm-up drills so I could make my lay-ups, grab my rebounds, and feed the next guy hustling through.

In a way it was like the Boys' Club, except the Boys' Club rarely drew more than a few dozen fans whose interest seemed to waver no matter how well we were doing. This was more like what I pictured it would be like with the Globetrotters. Would I ever make it? Well, I had made the high-school varsity as a freshman. But could I play? Would I improve?

Bouncing around during the warm-up with an undefeated team made me feel almost like I was really a part of it. I knew there were some in the stands who didn't know I was brand-new. I tried to carry myself as a full-fledged, season-long contributor.

Williston won that night, and easily. We were up by 20 with a couple of minutes to play, and the gym was rockin'. The whole school was excited about what was to be our twenty-ninth straight win. They could imagine a state championship, a perfect season. And so could I.

What I really wanted, though, was to get into the game. I wouldn't have to handle the ball, just let me jog out there and cover someone, give one of the seniors a break. If they passed to me, I'd pass it right back. I didn't want to show off. I just wanted to be part of it.

I had watched the game and the coaches intently and learned as much as I could soak up, but I wanted Coach Robinson to lean out and look down the bench and point to me. I wanted him to bark at me, "Lemon, get in there for. . . ."

But he didn't. Almost all the other subs were used, at least a little. That was all right. I didn't really expect to play that night. I just wanted to. I joined in the locker-room celebration, and I got slapped on the back by some of the regulars, as if I'd actually had something to do with the win. I knew better. So did they. I was there to learn and to prepare for next year. But I wondered when I would play, if not in an easy victory. Maybe in a big defeat? It didn't appear we would have any.

The next game was the same. A big, easy victory at home. I sat closer to the coaches on the bench, trying to make my presence obvious. I hoped maybe they'd remember that I was on the team and should get a little time on the floor, if it wouldn't be too much trouble. But I was ignored. That was all right. It really was. I knew there were more important things to this team than my getting a few minutes of playing time.

In fact, the next game was a road game against Laurinburg Institute with the legendary Sam Jones. Laurinburg had another advantage. They were a private school, so they recruited their athletes like a college team, from all over the country. I could forget about that game. Laurinburg Institute had lost one game in an upset to a weaker team, and they were ranked second in the state, right behind us.

Their gym was full of fans whose cheers almost seemed to raise the roof. When Laurinburg hit the floor, they had blood in their eyes. They wanted us. They knew that a victory would at least make them switch places with us in the rankings, and a big win might push us even lower. I think they expected to play us in the postseason tournaments that led to the state championship, and the winner of this game would take a big psychological advantage into that one.

Even during warm-ups, I found it hard to keep my eyes off Sam Jones, Laurinburg's outstanding junior. He was big, quick, fast, mobile, smart, and nonchalant. At least until game time. From the opening tip, he was all those things except nonchalant. Laurinburg Institute was a big team, and they meant to dominate us and run us ragged. Jones was one of those who made it happen for Laurinburg, playing both guard and forward as needed. He was a pure shooter.

Somehow, we scrambled and scratched to stay close, and at the half we were down by just 6. I had the best seat in the house. I could see Sam Jones pounding up and down the court, his dark skin glistening, sweat pouring from him. His head was up, his eyes bright. He was in shape and at the top of his game, a high-school junior with an NBA Hall of Fame future. He was like a thoroughbred.

In the locker room, Coach Robinson adjusted a little strategy, fixed a few things that weren't working, and convinced us we could beat this team. "A couple of breaks and we're *up* by 6. Let's not try to make it all up at once."

It was an understated pep talk, but it was effective. Our regulars took to the court with a new attitude in the second half, won the tip, and scored quickly. We were down by 4. Laurinburg Institute missed a shot, and we got the rebound, scored, and added a foul shot. We were down by 1. We fouled their shooter on the next trip down the court, but he missed both free throws. We could feel the momentum turning our way. I found myself sweating in my warm-up jacket. What a game!

At the end of the court, our sub center went up for a shot. Jones came over from his forward spot and went up with him, cleanly batting the ball away. They both came down reaching for the ball, but our man turned an ankle and went down in a heap. The ball skittered out of bounds, was awarded to Laurinburg, and time was called.

Coach Corbin and our student equipment manager, Joe, hurried out to check on our center. It didn't look too bad, but he had to be helped to the bench. The player next to me slapped me on the knee, but I was watching the injured player. "Lemon!" The guy on my other side leaned into me with his shoulder to get my attention. I looked at him. He was pointing at the other end of the bench.

I looked the other way, and the guy who slapped my knee kicked at my ankle and pointed at Coach Robinson. He was pointing at me, his expression grim because he couldn't get my attention. In the confusion I didn't know what he wanted. Maybe he was mad at me for not paying attention.

I looked at him, eyes wide, eyebrows up.

"Lemon! Get in there! Center!"

It was as if my life flashed before me and I realized that I was a football player. I didn't know anything about basketball! I had played at the club, sure, but Sam Jones? What? Where? How? I stood, rubbery legged. Coach Robinson was serious. He had already sat back down, expecting me to get in the game, just like anyone would whose coach had pointed at him. I charged onto the court, only to have Coach Corbin reach out and yank me back by my warm-up jacket. Oh, yeah. Got to take that off. I drew it over my head and let it fall. Coach Corbin tried to calm me, speaking softly, reassuringly. "Their ball. You're on defense under the hoop."

I raced to the hoop, my legs and my arms feeling like they belonged to someone else. *Why do my knees pump so high? Do I always run like this? Is everybody watching, or just almost everybody?* I had to get my mind on their center! *Let's see. Nothing fancy. Just deny him the ball.* But here they came, up the floor, moving the ball fluidly.

Their center wasn't looking at me. Did he know we had substituted? Did he care that there was a new man in? Did he wonder what abilities I might have? He swept through the lane. They passed to him! I reached out to bat the pass away, but I was late. He was going from my right to my left. I stepped out to take the charge, but he spun back to my right and was behind me. *I should foul him, anything to keep him from an easy basket.* Too late. The ball was dropping through.

I didn't even have time for an expression of disgust with myself. My teammates had taken the ball out and begun a fast break, which I found myself watching from behind. Realizing that I had to get into position for any of our set plays to work, I bounded up the court, nearly charging a defender and brushing one of my own teammates. But what were our plays? What would we run? The other four were passing the ball around, and I was wondering if I was in the right place, whether I would get a pass, and what I would do with it if I did.

What I was supposed to do was outposition my man so my teammates wouldn't be intimidated by him. He manhandled me like a rag doll. He picked off a pass through the lane that I hadn't even seen. He popped an outlet pass to one of his guards, and they streaked down court with him right behind them. I had to get in front of him, but again I was too late.

I had been standing there watching it happen, and he had three strides on me. I made a panicky effort to catch up with him. He caught the ball and sailed through the lane for a basket with me at his back. Then it was back to the other end. I was whipped already, and the second half was barely under way.

We were down by 5, and the weakest man on our team was

man-to-man against the strongest on theirs, maybe one of the strongest in the state. He ate me for breakfast, lunch, dinner, and dessert, all while hardly looking at me. I was simply in over my head and had little idea what to do.

The coach allowed me to embarrass myself for only about five minutes, then rested me on the bench for five more. When he sent me back in, nothing had changed. Laurinburg counted on Jones as a rule, regardless who the other team threw against him, but with a skinny freshman who was clearly outclassed, they just kept dishing their center the ball. I was never in the right position, couldn't hold the ball a second after taking a pass before he slapped it away or stole it, was outpositioned on almost every rebound, and basically got flat beat.

With me as the major weak link on our team, the Laurinburg lead increased until we were blown out. Near the end, Coach Robinson was looking for a substitute for me. My tongue was dragging.

Once I was on the bench, I felt something building within me. It wasn't humiliation, though I was embarrassed. (I was glad the game wasn't being played at Williston.) No, what was happening inside was something that would affect my entire career.

Something told me that this disaster wasn't my fault. The coaches weren't blaming me. No one was. I felt bad. I wished I had more experience and ability, but I was young, I was learning, and I was in an impossible situation. It was a cruel joke to have to face superstars in my first varsity basketball game, but then that's what happened in football, too, against J. C. Caroline.

I learned that night exactly where my game was. I was a good neighborhood player. I knew some of the fundamentals, and my abilities were coming along, but only because I was being coached by men who believed in the demonstration technique. In the game, however, no one walked through anything. Everything was done by instinct. And from that standpoint, I really didn't know basketball.

In my sleep I could see the Laurinburg center taking a pass, switching hands, countering my defense seemingly without thinking. He could outrun me, outjump me, outrebound me, outshoot me, and not all because of physical talent. He was a big man, sure, but it was his flat-out knowledge of the instinctive game.

He had been there before. He didn't have to think about it. He knew it cold down to his toes, and he acted and reacted from memory. In trying to talk myself through the game, I found myself on the short stick every time. What I needed, I came to realize, was more time in the gym, more laps, more shots, more drills, more game situations.

It took an in-your-face style of basketball to wake me up to exactly where I was and what I needed. I wanted to play ball at this level. No one blamed me for not being ready yet. I was the only halfway tall kid they had. No one else could have done any better, though I doubt they would have done worse either.

It had been a lot to ask of a green freshman to even stand in there, and I sensed that the coaches and my teammates appreciated my trying. I was glum, but I hadn't quit. I was determined. I was awakened. There was no reason I couldn't develop those skills, that quickness, that timing, that instinctive ability. I assumed my coaches knew what they were talking about, and I decided that from that point on whatever they asked me to do, I would do twice as much.

Some would think of me as coach's pet. Some would think I was crazy. Some would think I was trying to make everyone else look bad or lazy. But I knew the truth. I wasn't trying to make up for my performance. I simply believed that to succeed as a basketball player—and that meant nothing less than becoming a Harlem Globetrotter someday—I was going to have to make the most of my body and my mind.

Somehow, even at that age when most kids are wondering about their self-worth anyway, I think I had myself fairly accurately assessed. I knew I didn't have much natural ability. I had certain gifts, like the long arms and big hands, but everything else would have to be developed.

For those areas where I had some control, like conditioning, memorizing the fundamentals, and becoming an instinctive player, it was up to me. I became a madman in practice. If the coaches told us to jog ten laps, I'd sprint twenty. If they said to shoot until you made ten free throws in a row, I'd stay there till I made twenty. When everyone else went in for a shower, I stayed out and shot and shot and shot and shot.

The hook was nice and fun and someday would give me an edge, especially when I realized that if I shot it from much deeper out, the defense wouldn't even expect it. But I knew I needed a complete game. I wanted to develop a long game, a short game, an inside game, an outside game, a man-to-man game and a zone game, a strong offense, and a flypaper defense.

There was something about the way the Trotters had played ball—I had seen that short newsreel only once—that seemed to transcend normal basketball. It was as if they were able to do all those fun things, not just the gags and routines but also the behind-the-back passes, the through-the-leg dribbles, and the slam dunks, because the rest of their game was as instinctive as Sam Jones's.

That would be the type of game I would have to develop to reach my goal, and nothing was going to stand in the way of that. I didn't know how long it would take, but I knew I would get at least a few more chances to measure myself against the best before I was through.

I have been player-coach of two comedy basketball teams, the Bucketeers and, most recently, the Shooting Stars.

My bedroom window was the upper right one in my father's house at the corner of Sixth and Bladen in the Brooklyn section of Wilmington, North Carolina.

Ruby Bess was my seventh grade teacher, and her husband ran the Boys' Club for many years.

A picture of me in my first year with the Eastern Unit, the big team.

The Trotters ride a Ferris wheel in Germany.

Pulling reems in my second year on the Eastern unit.

The Globetrotters during a tour of Europe in my second year. I'm the dude with the hat in the back.

*The Lead Clown, Meadowlark
Lemon, dressed for a gag in
Scotland.*

The Globetrotters visit the Boys Town in Rome, Italy.

The Trotters perform a "five-ball spin" on the "Ed Sullivan Show."

Harmony on the Harlem Globetrotters. Give the famed basketball team a piano, and they'll swing into some fancy "barber shop" warbling. I'm the man on the keyboard.

Meadowlark and Abe. Even fools the boss. Meadowlark Lemon, new comedy sensation of the Harlem Globetrotters, unlooses a bit of his tomfoolery on Owner-Coach Abe Saperstein.

One of my favorite gags. David Lattin and Curly Neal help the "injured" clown prince off the court.

Me and "My Kids," a promotional photo for my "My Kids" record.

My role as the Reverend Jackson in the movie The Fish That Saved Pittsburgh.

Meadowlark Lemon's Bucketeers.

I always wanted to be a cowboy, so riding horses is a favorite hobby of mine.

Members of the Shooting Stars welcome Nancy Reagan as #1 on our team.

E. A. Corbin was the assistant basketball coach at Williston High School where I was grounded in the fundamentals. He remains one of my dearest friends.

At the top you can see the original name of the school, what it was called when I was in high school. Tradition said that seniors sat on the steps before school, but I was always too busy.

Curly Neal has remained a faithful friend since our early days together with the Globetrotters.

8

"I Will See You in Philippi!"

I began spending all my spare time at Coach Corbin's place. Earl Jackson from the Boys' Club brought his friend Henry, who could cook a mean mess of beans and hot dogs, and we spent all day Saturdays out there at the coach's place, doing yard work, eating, playing basketball, working on moves, fakes, hook shots, and defense. For some reason, I'd rather be there or at the high-school gym working out than even at home.

After practice on week nights, everyone else showered and went home, teasing me as they left. I stayed, shooting. Coach Corbin drove home for dinner, but often he'd come back for a little office work. Usually, I was still there. He'd shake his head and yell some encouragement that would offset the remarks from my teammates. They didn't mean anything by it. Maybe they wished they had my freedom so they could stay, too.

The problem was, my freedom had its good and bad sides. The extra time allowed me to devote myself to sports, including playing pickup games against kids from the white school, New Hanover High. We never played each other in sanctioned competition, but our practice fields were adjacent, and from the time I was fifteen, I had played against some of the best white players in North Carolina. They had won the state basketball championship the year before. There was some tension in the games, but not like you'd expect. It was probably the best training I got for my future as a black entertainer-athlete in a predominantly white world.

We played sandlot football against the white kids and even

some college kids who would come back for a little action. You grow up quick when you're playing seniors and collegians, especially with the added pressure of mixing the races, which simply wasn't to be done back then.

I also had the freedom to choose my friends, even my religion. I felt a need for some sort of an approach to God. I didn't know what I needed or wanted, but some of my friends were Catholics, so during high school I attended the Catholic church. Certain deep longings and desires were almost met there. I had the sense that we were trying to make contact with God. What Jesus and Mary and anyone else had to do with the whole scene I never quite figured out. What little catechism I got obviously didn't sink in. I wasn't very devout, but for a while there, I was a regular church attender. My father didn't attend, but he didn't mind my going.

Though Dad didn't like me wasting time harmonizing with the guys on the street corners after dark, I was free to join the high-school glee club, which at Williston Industrial was called the CORE club. Sonny Boy Jacobs got me interested in it. He went mostly to be around the girls.

In the CORE club I sang bass and competed with another guy to see who could sing lowest. I didn't realize it when I joined, but it became another good bit of training and preparation for me. The club traveled throughout several states during my high-school years, and we were expected to dress and act like well-behaved kids. At Christmas we sang over the Armed Forces Radio Network, and we heard back from some Wilmington boys stationed in Korea who had heard us. That, for some reason, warmed me deeply, and I felt as proud of having been involved in that as I was with any athletic achievement so far.

The basketball season ended with a sputter, all our early hopes and dreams dashed with an even record the rest of the way. Still, I was playing regularly, and while everyone knew it was simply because the other two centers were out, I was known around the school as the only freshman who had been a varsity starter in two sports.

I liked the notoriety and the popularity that went with it. I was shy but quick with a smile or a joke, and I did start to talk to the girls, even if I didn't have the courage yet to ask one out. I got to thinking I was pretty hot stuff, but as I said, the freedom I enjoyed had its down side, too.

Lots of older guys hung around the basketball games and the team members. We looked up to these "graduates," so when one of them named Alan asked me to go to a nightclub one Sunday evening, I said sure. I knew all they did there were things I wasn't supposed to do as an athlete in training, but I was feeling my oats. I was big time, getting well known. I could handle it. I was just going to observe.

Alan brought a bottle of Old Crow in a brown paper sack and kept hitting on it for the first half-hour we were there. I was getting bored and uncomfortable and must have looked like I wanted to get out of there. Alan was old enough to order beer from the bar, but all I could do was sit and watch people dance, listen to the music, and wonder if any card games were going to get out of hand. It was a dead end. I was bored.

Alan thought he had the solution. "What you need, my man, is to get high." He held out the bottle.

I waved him off. "Nah, man, I don't drink. You know that."

"What'sa matter, little Meadow, is it past your bedtime, hm?"

"Alan, I don't drink, and I don't intend to start. My dad would kill me, not to mention my coaches."

"Oh, are they your baby sitters? C'mon, little Meadow. Are you still a little bitty baby?"

I ignored him and looked away, disgusted.

"Are you chicken, Meadow?"

"Of course not."

"Then come on. One little shot ain't gonna hurt you. Here."

Like a fool, I took it, telling myself it was just to pacify him and to prove I was man enough. I tipped it back and then brought it down, but only a little whiskey actually stayed in my mouth. I wiped my lips with the back of my hand and gave the bottle back.

Alan held up both hands and whispered, "No, man, you got to say, 'Ahhh!' If you don't say, 'Ahhh!' it don't do you no good." He pushed the bottle into my hands.

I made a face and put the bottle back up to my lips. I tipped it back and let seven or eight big swallows roll down my throat. I didn't feel anything more than I'd felt when I took the swig. At least at first. The bottle was more than half-empty when I handed it back, and then the room started to swim.

My eyes filled, my throat burned, my stomach churned, my head buzzed. If this was a high, I was soaring. I felt like my body was on fire. I stared at Alan. "Oh, man, I don't think I should have done that."

He chuckled. "You're just not used to it."

I thought the feeling would pass. When it didn't, I started to panic. "Man, I really feel bad. My throat and stomach are burning. Get me some water."

"What you need is a chaser."

"I know. Water!"

He got me some, but it was lukewarm and didn't do the trick. I moaned, held my stomach, and tried to suck in enough air to relieve my throat. Alan was eager to help. "Hang on. A beer will get rid of that feeling."

He came back in a minute with a huge mug of ice cold beer. It sure looked good. If ever there was a medicinal drink, I assumed this was it. I was getting sicker by the minute, and I saw that mug as an oasis in the desert.

I eagerly cupped it in both hands and held it up to my lips. I don't know if I was expecting root beer or what, but the smell was slightly bitter, pungent. I didn't care. The glass was frosty, and the condensation ran down my fingers. This would definitely cool my parched throat, and I only hoped it would do the same for my stomach.

I never stopped to think that it was more booze than I had drunk the first time. The foam brushed my nose, and the cool balm hit my mouth. Ah! Relief. The farther I tipped that mug, the better my mouth and throat felt. I drank the whole thing down before taking a break. It tasted awful, but that wasn't the point. For a split second my throat felt better. My stomach felt worse.

Then I realized I was in trouble. I couldn't see straight. I couldn't think. I knew I was in a place I shouldn't be in, with a person I shouldn't be with, doing something I shouldn't be doing. I was sick. I tried to stand and bumped against the wall. "I—I—I've got, I've gotta get home, uh, Alan."

"You're all right, Slick. Sit down."

"No!" I was slurring already. Disoriented. "I gotta get outa here, man."

I tried to walk out, but I bumped into people and fell twice. I felt Alan's head under my arm. He dragged me out to the street and flagged down a cab. Then Alan was gone. The cabby turned around and looked at me. "Ain't you Peanut Lemon's boy?"

I nodded, groaning.

He headed toward my house. "Don't you be throwing up in my car, boy!"

"I'll try not." I cried from the pain.

That wasn't what he wanted to hear. He drove faster. When he heard one moan too many, he jerked the car to the curb. I looked out. "Three blocks more, sir."

"Oh, no, son. This is it! No charge, and you walk the rest of the way." He hurried around to my door and helped me out. He thought I was going to lose everything right there, and I almost did. "You can find your way now, Meadow?"

I nodded and staggered off. He sat and watched a while, then slowly drove away. I groaned when I got to the house. Dad was home. I could hope he was asleep and wouldn't be interested in my arrival. I came in the back as quietly as possible for a kid stone drunk.

As I got to the top of the stairs, I was ready to let fly. I rushed into my room, slammed the door, turned on the light, grabbed a pillowcase, and filled it. Five minutes later I couldn't find another container, so I filled a small heater.

I slept fitfully, due to the stench and my throbbing head, and then I must have more passed out than slept. In the morning I tried to wash away the smell that seemed to seep from my every pore. I felt awful.

I felt worse when I picked up my books and headed off to school. We were going to have the final in Mrs. Leonard's English class. I hadn't studied, and I was in no condition to take a final. Worse, I was convinced I smelled like a wino and that everyone could tell. I didn't hide my condition too well. I drew a lot of stares and snickers.

Mrs. Leonard's English class was right after homeroom, and already the news was getting around school that Meadow Lemon was hung over. Most wouldn't believe it until they saw me—or smelled me—but then they were convinced.

I had tried to peek at the English book during homeroom and on the way to class, but I was still disoriented. I didn't know what alcohol could do to a person, but I got a quick lesson. Mrs. Leonard took one look at me, stopped her final exam instructions, and asked me to follow her. How humiliating! I left the room to the sound of murmuring and giggling.

Mrs. Leonard—we sometimes called her Mother Leonard— had a big, high voice. She made no mention of the obvious reason for my condition. She just marched me straight into the boys' bathroom—she was also the type who had no qualms about that. "I've raised enough boys that nobody's gonna show me somethin' I haven't seen!"

She set my books on one sink and ran cold water in the other. Then she pushed my head down close to it and washed my face. She was surprisingly gentle and understanding, even though I was still terribly embarrassed. "Meadow, you're in no shape to be takin' a test today. I want you to go home and get some sleep. That's the only thing that works, you understand?"

I nodded gratefully.

"Now, understand me, boy. I hope this is a lesson for you."

"Yes, ma'am."

"And also, you will have to take this final sometime. Nobody graduates from this school without takin' the freshman English final, be they star athletes or straight-A students in everything else. You got that?"

"Yes, ma'am, and thank you."

"Don't you be thankin' me, now. You just get some rest, get better, and get back here for that exam, or you know what."

I nodded.

She said it anyway, "I will see you in Philippi!"

I hoped she would forget the exam, and for three long years, I thought she had. I became the most popular and well-known sports star in that school and did very well academically. But when we were practicing the processional march for graduation, not three days before our big day, here came Mrs. Leonard. She saw me in Philippi.

She came right up to me in the middle of the line and grabbed me by the ear. "Meadow Lemon, I don't care who you are or who you think you are or how big anybody else thinks you are. You will be takin' your freshman English final, or you won't need any marching practice."

She gave me a little while to study for it, put me in a freshman classroom where the kids were taking the same test, and I sat there and endured it. You can imagine how big I must have looked to those fourteen-year-olds.

I got a ninety-eight.

9

My Baseball "Career"

Reminiscing recently with Coach Corbin, I was humorously reminded of my short-lived high-school baseball career. During tryouts in the spring of my freshman year—not long after my first and last experience with alcohol (I haven't touched a drop since)—he and the assistant coaches had been amazed by my natural defensive abilities. Knowing I had been a varsity starter in two sports already, they assumed I was the answer to their need at first base.

I caught everything hit or thrown my way, and hitting seemed easy. That was because the pitchers were my teammates or coaches, and they were throwing easily. I didn't tell anyone that, in truth, I was afraid of the ball. I'd seen Larry Doby, first black player in the American League, get beaned, and I didn't want any part of it. If I hurt myself giving my all in basketball, that was one thing. To risk my future on a sport I enjoyed but didn't love was something else again.

Every day I rocketed line drives all over the field, and since I had developed good speed, I guess I was impressive on the basepaths, too. Coach gave me the starting job and put me third in the line-up. I didn't admit I was terrified.

We were the home team in the first game of the season. The first ball hit was a line drive at me. I instinctively flicked my glove at it and snagged it. I knew anyone could have done it, but people were impressed. They thought I was going to be a three-sport standout.

The next hitter grounded slowly to third. I raced to the bag and straddled it so I could touch it with either foot depending on where the throw came. Our third baseman barehanded the ball on the dead run and fired low and short. I knew if I waited for the high hop, the runner would beat the throw, so I put my right toe on the bag and stretched as far as I could with my left foot, reaching with my glove.

I was virtually doing the splits, but I got my glove out far enough to take the throw on the short hop, beating the runner by an eyelash. I enjoyed the applause, but I dreaded the idea of hitting against an enemy pitcher who would just as soon take my head off as look at me. I had seen him warming up. I prayed he would pitch in the game as lazily as he had tossed on the sidelines.

The next hitter drove a hard grounder to my left, just inside the bag. I went into shallow right field to glove it, turned all the way around to my right, and led the pitcher perfectly as he ran to cover first. Two putouts and an assist. Not a bad start.

The opposing pitcher was taller than he had appeared. He cut loose with a couple of fastballs at the end of his warm-up tosses that resounded across the field and almost took his catcher's glove off. I trembled.

Our leadoff man, the best hitter on our team, struck out on three fastballs, weakly fouling off the second and staring in disbelief at the other two white streaks. I thought I might have to go to the bathroom.

While I knelt in the on-deck circle taking practice swings and trying to time the pitcher's speed, our second hitter took a ball inside that made me hold my breath, then struck out on three pitches, the first two looking. For the record, I struck out in the on-deck circle.

Facing this pitcher made me feel like I was going to the dentist. I knew I had to do it, but the backs of my legs tingled and I feared for my life. I walked slowly into the batter's box, and some told me later they thought I looked calm and nonchalant. In fact, I was in a terrified trance.

This guy was a senior with major league scouts following his every move. Why did I always have to have such luck? The toughest pitching I had faced had been Richard Gillyard. I decided I would swing at whatever he threw to keep from prolonging the agony. I didn't want to take a pitch and risk it being a ball, giving him yet another opportunity to kill me.

I stood deep in the batter's box and far from the plate. If he threw at me, it would have to be deliberate. His first pitch came in high and hard and out over the plate, probably a better pitch than he intended to throw the number-three hitter. I was panicky and jumpy, but I had already decided to swing three times and get it over with. I stepped and lunged at the ball.

The bat recoiled as I made contact, and I'll never forget how heavy that ball felt from its incredible speed. It hit on the sweet part of the bat and screamed toward the right center field gap, rising as it went. The center fielder and the right fielder turned to watch it, but they didn't chase it. It was still rising as I sprinted around first, so scared and so excited I couldn't slow down and enjoy it.

If there had been a fence, the ball would have cleared it easily. As it was, it bounced twice and kept rolling. Somewhere between second and third, I made my decision. I had never quit anything before in my life, and as much as I loved and admired Coach Corbin, I didn't want to start now. But I was an impostor.

I didn't belong on this team. I could play defense, sure, that was a gift. But I was afraid of the pitching. I had power, that was clear, but the homer was luck. I couldn't kid myself. It might be ten more games before I got a bat on the ball again.

Between third and home I steeled myself against the pleading and the criticism I knew would come. My decision might not be rational, and it was certainly selfish, but it was also final.

I got a smack on the butt and a handshake from the third-base coach, and I met a group of four or five teammates at the plate. Coach Corbin was waiting for me in the dugout with a big smile and his hand extended.

"Congratulations, Meadows. So far you're batting a thousand."

"I also quit."

"What? You're kidding." He could see that I wasn't.

I picked up my glove. "The pitching's too fast for me. I'm sorry, but I'm done."

"Meadows, don't do this. You hit one out."

I was on my way to the locker room. I called over my shoulder, "Don't try to talk me out of it, Coach. I'm not kidding. I'm not ready for this, and I'm not gonna stand in against this pitching."

And I didn't. I stuck to it. For some reason, Coach Corbin didn't try to lay a guilt thing on me about letting the team down. He knew me better than that. I think he figured that if I felt strong enough to leave the field and the team after playing a flawless first inning and hitting a home run off a premier pitcher, I must have known what I was talking about.

I was the guy who worked with a tackling dummy at home during the football season, who worked out in the gym late every night and at the coach's house every weekend during the basketball season, and who ran most of the way to and from school every day to stay in shape for whatever sport I was in. Playing a good first base was not enough to really help a team. A fair fielder who could also hit would be better than a good-field, no-hit guy like me.

I was right, and he knew it. I don't know if my teammates ever figured it out, unless they watched me hit in summer leagues. I was such a good fielder it made my hitting look worse. A big league scout, at a game to watch someone else, told me that with the way I handled myself around first base, if I could even hit .200 in the big leagues, he'd sign me.

I said, "Me hit .200 in the big leagues? I ain't hittin' .180 in *this* league!"

He laughed and walked away.

Basketball was going to have to be my game.

That summer Wallace Keils, Edward Sutton, and I got a job cutting tobacco. We had never had to stand out in the sun all day, working hard. It was too much. We hid under a huge tobacco leaf for a little relief and quickly got real used to it.

The boss caught us. He could have been much tougher on us. He said, "Look, I want to give you boys a chance. I need your help, and you need the money. I know you're not used to this heat yet, so I'm going to give you the rest of the day off. Without pay, of course. But you're free to go now."

I knew if I left, I'd never come back, and I assumed the others felt the same way. I tried to reason with the man. "We don't have any money. And we're hungry."

"Well, I owe you half a day's pay." He paid us. "And I'll see you tomorrow, first thing."

Unless he's seen me play somewhere, that man hasn't seen me since.

Our plan was simply to work for the money we needed and then move on. All I needed was enough for train and bus tickets to Harlem. Sometimes that meant working at one of the beaches east of Wilmington—Wrightsville to the north and Carolina to the south. Wrightsville Beach was for the rich people, so the only thing a black high-school kid could do there *was* work. I ran the elevator at the resort there for a while and did some dishwashing, too.

The only time I could get into the water was at night, and I knew I'd better be out before daybreak. Ironically, after I had made it with the Trotters, I was welcome to go to the white Carolina Beach and to eat in restaurants I could have only worked in as a kid.

I started making it a regular spot when I visited home. Earl would drive me out there with whoever else we could round up from the old days, and we'd enjoy the man's all-you-can-eat seafood special. My old high-school teacher, Mrs. L. S. Williams—I'll tell a story about her later—asked me recently what my favorite seafood was. My answer was simple. "Seafood."

Once when I was back visiting, Earl and Son and I went to that place on Carolina Beach. Son ate like there was no tomorrow. He literally used his tray as a plate. No way that owner could have made a dime on us that night, all because of Son. On our way out, the owner was gracious. He was also firm.

"You know, Earl, I appreciate how much work you've done with the boys of this town. And you know how proud I am of Meadowlark. It's a privilege to have you bring him here whenever he's in town. You're always welcome here. But do me a favor." He gestured toward Son. "Don't ever bring this man in here again." He wasn't kidding.

10

All-State
in Football and Basketball

My sophomore year at Williston Industrial was my turnaround year. I was growing, and my confidence was high after being named to start on both offense and defense on the football team. Basketball season had just started when the announcement was made that I had been named to the all-state football team.

I knew I'd had a good year as a receiver and as a cornerback, but I certainly hadn't even considered being named all-state. Uncle Wash and Dad came to the games and bet people how many tackles, how many one-handed catches, and how many devastating blocks I'd make. Sometimes they came down to the bench and encouraged me, winking and showing me the money I'd won for them. I had to shoo them away.

I had to do that several years later when two of my uncles came to watch the Globetrotters play for the first time. We were doing the now-famous injury routine where I go down in a heap and have to be helped to the foul line. Then I shoot with a succession of gag basketballs. My uncles saw me go down and the other team pretending to have knocked me out. I guess my yelling didn't sound too amusing to my uncles, so they came barreling down out of the stands with knives drawn. Luckily, I saw them before most anyone else did and was able to calm them down and get them out of the way.

The basketball team at Williston my sophomore year was centered around four returnees: Willie Jacobs, Brokey Saunders, Robert Brooks, and me. So, it was Slim, Brokey, Sonny Boy, and Iron Man.

Brokey Saunders was a good ballhandler and shooter who got his name from a broken arm that was never set right and jutted out at an angle. (Playing superman as a child, he thought his cape would keep him up if he jumped off the garage.) He could do things with that arm that no normal kid could do, but he suffered the rest of his high-school career being called Brokey.

Coaches Robinson and Corbin had us help them scout and recruit up-and-coming basketball players so we could build a decent team. We came up with a pretty good group. Eddie Jacobs was the showoff, throwing garbage or school-yard shots.

Maurice Graham was the biggest guy on the team, but he didn't show much mobility or aggressiveness until very late in his high-school days. Bap Boyd, one of the Hometown Boys from my neighborhood in Brooklyn, was the smallest on our team, but he played some good ball for us.

My back-up man was Tee Harvey, a great baseball player and a fair basketball player. Many thought I was the best player on the team once I came into my own that second year, but I would have given the nod to Iron Man Brooks. He was something to watch.

He wasn't that tall, but he was wide and muscular and powerful. Amazingly, he could play guard, handling and passing the ball and running the offense. He could play forward, picking up rebounds and scoring when necessary. And he could play center. He was the most complete athlete I've ever seen. Everything came so naturally, he was like a machine.

That was the year I really learned to fake and get some of the important nuances into my game. Coach Corbin taught me to counteract a bigger defender by making him go up with a fake, then driving into his outstretched arms on the shot. We both knew the foul should be called on the shooter, but there isn't one referee in ten who'll call it that way.

Williston hadn't beaten Rocky Mount High in years, so the coaches really had us up for that road game. I faked their star player so bad on one play that he lunged and hit the wall, claiming I had charged him. That little argument almost broke out in a fight, but the official was right there. He had seen it. I had faked the man, he had made his move, and neither of us got anything but air. The ball got hoop, however. We won.

One night we played in a little bandbox of a gym in Southport. The rickety old court had a wrought iron, potbellied stove that blazed continuously to warm the icy night. Poles at either end of the floor supported the backboards, and the Southport boys had learned to slam dunk, using those without the refs noticing (or caring). They would go up at full speed with the ball palmed in one hand, grabbing the pole with the other and propelling themselves high above the rim.

The local principal made a prediction. He told our coaches, "Our team is ready for Lemon and Saunders. We're gonna neutralize 'em. They won't do a thing."

Mr. Robinson and Mr. Corbin took him seriously. We had quite a reputation, and it wouldn't have been so unusual for them to have been planning all week how to stop Brokey and me from scoring so much.

Our coaches had an idea. "We're going to start a couple of subs for Lemon and Saunders and maybe not play them until the second half, maybe not even until the fourth quarter. If Southport has been practicing all week to stop them, they won't know what to do when they're not in. Then, when we've run them ragged, we'll bring in our stars and really give 'em a show."

Brokey and I were averaging over 20 points each per game, so we weren't too excited about the plan. But we were team players, and the coaches assured us that when we did get in, we could trade off scoring all we wanted. The plan worked like a charm.

Southport was so confused and frustrated, they couldn't do anything right. And our back-up men were so happy to be starting, they played above their heads and did outstanding jobs. Brokey and I didn't play a minute until the fourth quarter when we already had a 10-point lead.

The starters on both teams were dragging by then, and we played as fresh as we felt. It was as if everyone else was in slow motion. I don't know if it's ever been done before or since—it was certainly rare in those days—but Williston scored 51 points in the last quarter, all by Brokey and me, and we held the opposition to one field goal and one free throw. We had confounded their strategy and kept our averages intact, too.

The night came, of course, when we got our rematch against Sam Jones and Laurinburg Institute. They had beaten us by 1 point at their place, and we had blood in our eyes for the next rematch, this time at home.

Fortunately for us, Iron Man was healthy. He had one assignment: Forget everything but muscling Jones away from the ball and the basket. Deny him position, deny him the ball, deny him the shot. Let Meadow and Brokey handle the scoring.

What a game!

Brooks was all over Jones like stink on a pig. Once Jones was so frustrated he tried to run right through Iron Man, and they both crashed through a pair of doors at the end of the gym. We waited and waited for them to finally stagger back in from the ice and snow. You could see their breath as they slapped each other on the back.

When it was all over, we had won by 1 point. Brokey and I had scored a couple of dozen each. Iron Man contributed 4, and he held Jones to just below his average. Whew, we enjoyed that!

I wish I could point to one day when my game came together and I knew I was going to be a standout. Of course, I had believed all along that it had to happen. If it didn't, I could forget my Globetrotter dream. There were times when I wondered, but I always had faith in myself. I wanted it badly enough to pay the price, and gradually, the hard work and determination began to pay off. I was scared to death to quit learning and growing in the game. The better I got, the more I worked because more was expected of me. Something also told me that every time I moved up a level, I was going to feel like a beginner again. I wanted to be ready.

I felt confident on the court. I felt natural. I could see every player on both teams and could sense plays developing. I found myself in the right place at the right time on both offense and defense, and yet it wasn't luck. I had invested hours in getting to this point. I didn't take it for granted, and I never coasted.

Our team made the final sixteen in the state that year, and I was named all-state. With that came more popularity than I had ever had, but I got used to it very quickly. My confidence on the court boosted my confidence off the court, and suddenly, I found it easier to talk to girls. They knew who I was, and they actually *wanted* to talk to me! That was something new.

In spite of foolish advice from my friends (for instance, Wallace Keils's philosophy was that a man should give his woman a whuppin' once a week whether she deserves it or not!), I instinctively acted like a gentleman around girls. They seemed to appreciate that. I don't know if it was gentlemanly of me to mooch food off them, like Chester Green swears I did, but who can believe a guy who eats his lunch in the bathroom to run from the girls?

I was a little embarrassed because one of the girls who caught my eye was actually the younger sister of a girl who was a year behind me in school. It was one thing for a sophomore to date a freshman, but to be interested in a junior higher, that was taboo. But Ophelia Maultsby's little sister was a knockout. Her name was Willye, and she had a beautiful little round face with the most gorgeous complexion. I couldn't tell a soul how I felt about her.

From that point on, my dedication and confidence in high-school sports carried me to greater heights. I don't recall becoming bigheaded—that problem would come later—but I had a quiet self-assurance that helped my game. I knew I was still the type of player who would always have to work at it, but I was more than willing to do that.

I found that my jumping ability and timing had allowed me to play taller than I really was. Taller people were too slow to stay with me, and people my height or shorter were too small to defend against me. That, with all the fundamentals being drilled into me, contributed to the ballplayer I became.

By the time I was a senior, I was one of the best-known students at the school, and I enjoyed every minute of it. I was into a lot of activities, but the only one I really cared about was basketball.

I still had my eye on little Willye Maultsby, but I didn't dare tell her or anyone else. I had enough other things on my mind, like all the colleges and universities that began writing and offering me full scholarships in football and basketball, some in both.

I honestly didn't know if I wanted to go to college. Would I like it? Would I succeed? Most important, would it help or hinder me in attaining my goal? I couldn't think about it. There was still a lot of high-school basketball to be played, and it looked as if we might have a shot at the state championship.

To really test us, the coaches arranged a two-game set against the junior varsity at Shaw University, an all-black school, in Raleigh. They would play us at home, then we would play them at their place. In the game just prior to the first one against them, I took an elbow in the eye that forced me to sit out.

I can't tell you how devastated I was. It was bad enough that I couldn't play basketball, but I had been so eager to be tested by older competition. Some of those players were on college basketball scholarships. Okay, they weren't on the varsity yet, but they would be someday. How I wanted to play! Many of the teachers at our school were alumni of Shaw, and the game drew an enormous crowd.

With Brokey and Iron Man in there, somehow we beat them anyway. Our gym was rockin', and you could tell the Shaw team was humiliated, even though we had won by just 1 point. They had not expected to find us even interesting competition.

Several weeks later, I was healthy and averaging better than 30 points a game. It was time to play Shaw again, this time on their court. The word was out. They were stocking their junior varsity with stars from their varsity. No way they wanted to lose to a high-school team in their own field house. Well, I wanted competition. *This* would be interesting. Our ace in the hole was that they had not faced me before.

I couldn't wait.

11

The One-Handed Shot
That Never Was

The game in Raleigh against Shaw University was the first really great basketball game I ever played. Scoring more than 20 points in the fourth quarter of the Southport game had showed me the possibilities, but that was in a crackerbox against a weak high-school team.

People showed up for this game. I mean, they really showed up. Word had gotten around that Shaw had had its highly touted junior varisty humbled by a high-school team, so not just university students but also the townspeople came out to see the rematch. The press was there, too.

I was psyched, but not just because of the crowd. I was fully aware that it was a platform, an arena where I could show my stuff, but I wasn't thinking about that as much as the test itself. Shaw couldn't have thrilled me more than to put varsity stars in the game. I didn't know how well I'd do, but something told me this was a very big opportunity.

My secret was that Shaw University was recruiting me. Few people knew about that, but they had been quietly asking questions and encouraging me to think of them in the future. I really wanted to show them now.

I wasn't expected to do well. Everyone knew Shaw was stacking their team and intended to show us that our previous win was a fluke. In that sense, the pressure was off. But ever since the first high-school game I had ever played, the one where Laurinburg Institute mopped the floor with me, I had eagerly sought stiffer competition.

The game against Laurinburg had showed me exactly where my game was, what I needed to work on. And I had done that. It had resulted in two straight years of all-state awards and a feeling that I was really getting somewhere. If someone had told me to stand in against George Mikan, the giant center of the National Basketball Association's Minneapolis Lakers, I'd have jumped at the chance.

Could I have competed? I had no idea. I doubted it. But the test was the thing. There was so much to be learned, so much to gain. (A few years before, on February 20, 1948, the Harlem Globetrotters were challenged to play the NBA powerhouse, Mikan-led Lakers. The game was held in Chicago, played straight, and the Trotters won, 61-59. I couldn't have been more thrilled. Later that year, the Lakers became NBA champions, proving to me at least that the Globetrotters were the best team in America. A few of my friends had wondered how I could be so impressed with a team that, they said, was more clown than class, more comedy than talent. Maybe now they understood.)

I was so excited by the time we hit the court for warm-ups in Raleigh, I could hardly stand it. I couldn't even buy a lay-up. I was passing over everyone's head, dribbling too hard, breathing too heavily. Ooh, I just wanted to get on with the game. Coach Corbin, always a picture of dignity, stood watching me from near the bench, his arms folded across his chest, his look solemn.

When we came in to strip down to our uniforms and get last-minute instructions, he stepped out and put a hand on my shoulder. "Harness it, son. Harness it. Direct it to the game."

I nodded. I knew what he meant. I would be no good to the team the way I was. It wouldn't pay to have me trying to do things that weren't even within my capabilities. I was intense, on a natural high. I had to focus. In the second before the opening tip-off, I did. I ran through my mind all that would have to happen for us to upset this older, more experienced team. We had to be faster, smarter, more accurate, and more creative.

The game itself is a blur in my memory. All I remember is stealing the ball a half-dozen times, firing outlet passes to start the fast break, rebounding with big men, dribbling with the guards, passing, ballhandling, shooting as if the game had been made for me.

It was one of those nights that, for most people, comes along once in a lifetime. I'm happy to say that with the thousands of games I've played since, the law of averages has provided a few more just like it for me, but that night was my first experience.

It seemed I couldn't miss a shot, and when I did, the rebound came to me for the tip-in. I made all but one free throw and shot nearly 70 percent from the field. I scored 45 points, but the game was close, neck and neck all the way. I could feel the awe of the other players and the fans, even though they were pulling for Shaw. By the end of the third quarter, my success with shots from all over the court was almost becoming funny. My teammates just started feeding me every time up the court, and even though Shaw knew I was coming, they couldn't stop me.

Time seemed to stand still. When I went up for a shot, I was a foot over everyone. Occasionally, when they jumped in a futile attempt to block, I hung onto the ball and shot on the way down, bumping their hands and turning it into a 3-point play. I was playing the way I dreamed I would play one day with the Harlem Globetrotters.

By the end, when every basket traded the lead by a point, everyone was clapping and cheering for me. I even noticed that some of the opposition were shaking their heads. I felt as if I'd died and gone to heaven. If I had never played basketball again as long as I lived, that game would have been worth it. Except my dream was still alive. In fact, more alive than ever.

With five seconds on the clock, Shaw scored to go up by 1. Our guard had a tough time getting the ball in, but we were out of time-outs. Finally, he bounced a pass to me. I had enough time to move farther up court, but I didn't want to risk not getting a shot off. The pass hit me in midstride, and everything felt right, even though I was three-quarters of the length of the floor from the basket.

I dribbled once and pushed up a running one-handed shot that arced high and deep and quieted that crowd in an instant. The place just went dead silent. I hopped and skipped, following the shot, because it felt so good. It was straight on. All I wondered was whether I had gotten enough power behind it. My intention was to bank it in off the backboard. It swished, popping the net as the horn sounded.

Our team was in pandemonium! We had done it! But here came the president of Shaw University. He bounded over the press table onto the floor and signaled, just like a referee, that the shot was no good. "Time had expired! Time had expired!"

Everyone knew he was wrong. I looked to the refs, who were (of course) from that area. Suddenly, they were mirror images of him, signaling that the shot was too late. The Shaw fans cheered, but they knew better. Everyone did. My shot had shut them up so everyone heard the buzzer sound as the shot dropped through, not before, and certainly not before I let it go.

I felt a huge arm around my neck. The Shaw coach had collared me on the run. He was furious. "You can forget about playing ball here, Lemon. I don't go for all that hot dog Globetrotter stuff!"

Later it was rumored that a Harlem Globetrotter scout saw one of my high-school games. I was never able to get that confirmed, but I'd like to think that it was that game. Either that or our last game of the season, which was another wild one. I was averaging over 29 points per game, and I was hoping for a good game to push myself over 30 for the season.

The coaches had other ideas. We had already qualified for the play-offs and had handily won our conference. In our last regular season game, we played a Beaufort team so weak that they had asked permission to combine their players with the players from another small local school. In essence, we played the area's all-star team.

Coaches Robinson and Corbin wanted everybody to get a chance to play, so the regulars didn't even start. I wasn't terribly disappointed, especially after I saw how bad the competition was. There wasn't much fun in beating a weak team, especially when you wanted to keep testing yourself against the best.

By the end of the first half, with the score 40–6 in favor of our subs, the crowd began to leave. Beaufort's coach asked Coach Robinson if there was anything he could do. Robinson was at a loss. "I'm sorry, but our regulars are on the bench as it is. I don't know if we could let up any more unless I told my kids to quit shooting. I even suited up Joe, our equipment manager, who has never even practiced with us before. *He's* been scoring."

Coach Robinson thought a moment. "I've got an idea. Wait here a moment," he added as he turned away from the Beaufort coach.

He walked over to me. "Hey, Meadow, what about trying some of those trick shots you fool around with during practice?"

When I looked surprised, he reassured me. "Don't worry about humiliating this team. They know what they're up against."

That was all I needed to hear. I pretended I was Goose Tatum. I cackled and yelled and cavorted, streaking up and down the court, dribbling between my legs, passing behind my back, slam dunking, you name it. I had another 40-plus game, this time in just one half. We scored 85 points in the second half and ran the score up to 125–20. It was fun, and the crowd loved it. Many who had left at half time came back to see what was going on.

We were favored to win the state championship, but we were worried. Something was going wrong with Iron Man. He was missing easy shots and seemed to be losing his bearing on and off the court. In practice, and sometimes even in games, he missed and would laugh hysterically. Then he might break down and cry. No one could draw him out to find out what was wrong.

One day no one could find me. I had become a good student and a good school citizen, so the coaches found it hard to believe I would skip school. I hadn't intended to. It was just that before school someone said they assumed I had already seen the Globetrotter movie down at the Bijou Theater.

"Yeah, I saw a newsreel about six years ago, but I only saw it once."

"No, Lemon, this is a whole movie starring the Globetrotters. It's called *The Harlem Globetrotters*."

"It's down there now?"

"It was yesterday."

I was gone. I didn't tell or ask anyone. If there had ever been a good reason to play hooky, this was it. I went alone, and I sat there all day. That team traveled by bus almost everywhere they went.

They had a little white owner and coach whom they all seemed to love, and what fun they had. They *were* a family, just as I had suspected.

All the old feelings returned. I couldn't get enough of it. I could see why that brief glimpse when I was eleven had stayed with me through the years, convincing me that I wanted to be a Globetrotter above all else. If that feeling could intensify, the full-length feature had done it.

After that, I didn't care who knew my ambition. I couldn't quit talking about the movie, the Trotters, Goose Tatum. People could make fun all they wanted—most didn't, because it was clear now that I had ability—and it didn't faze me. I was on course. I didn't know how or when, but I was going to make it. They would all see.

Had I known what the odds were or what the competition would be, I might have wavered. They say ignorance is bliss. In my case, ignorance was determination.

Williston Industrial made it all the way to the final four in the state tournament. We had close games all the way, closer than they should have been. Teams we had beat by 20 points during the season were taking us to the wire, mostly because Iron Man couldn't see the basket. That's what he said. That he couldn't see it. We were worried. His vision was checked. Normal.

He was supposed to do his thing, clog up the middle, muscle the opposition, free Brokey and me up to do what we did best. But lately he was doing a lot of nothing except missing shots and complaining that he couldn't see the basket.

In the semifinal game, he came unraveled. He cried. He broke down. He had to be helped from the court. He was institutionalized, and that was the last most of us ever heard of him. We lost. It would be years before Williston had a team as good. In the early 1970s, they finally won a state basketball title. When I think of what might have been. . . . We wanted it so bad. We couldn't blame poor Iron Man. Something just came loose.

High school without basketball was something different. I was having fun, trying to hold on to my high-school year as long as I could, knowing my dad wanted me to go to college and wanting to be a Globetrotter above all else. Dad said that with all the free ride offers I was getting, I'd be a fool to pass up a college education.

I just wanted to have fun for a while. My favorite teacher that final year was Mrs. L. S. Williams, a big, dominating woman who taught English and intimidated everyone. We said that she had eyes in the back of her head—no talking, no lookin' under the girls' dresses. I could never sneak in late, even when her back was to the door. In her high, powerful voice, she'd call me down. She'd say, "Son, I love you like a brother, but if you don't start gettin' to my class on time, I'll flunk you down, just like I did my brother!"

That was a woman so powerful that when she sat down, rather than scooting her chair up to the desk, she pulled the desk toward her! We called her Big Wheel, and she remembers that we said she was "mean as a dog." I visit her when I get back to Wilmington. She's now a dear eighty-year-old who lives in a house she has lived in since she was two. It's decorated with old furniture from her childhood and looks immaculate.

When I visited her not long ago, she told me how excited she was after I called ahead. "God bless your heart, you made my day. Yes, yes, yes. I wasn't walkin' worth a cent the last week, but after your phone call, I was walkin' all over the place. I had to get the T.I.B. and the H.I.B. so I could be ready. Yes, yes."

"Your what?"

She giggled. "The teeth I bought and the hair I bought! I put on everything. I'm so glad to see you, bless your heart."

Some years after I had left town and become a Globetrotter, Mrs. Williams remembered that I had not had enough money to buy my high-school annual when I graduated. I got her tickets to come and see our game, and she presented me with the annual for my senior year. Quite a woman. Yes, yes. When I was back there recently, my old friends and I were reminiscing about her.

Chester Green remembered that I was the one who used to egg him on when he had an argument with Mrs. Williams. "Nine times out of ten, Meadow would get me thrown out of the room, and Mrs. Williams didn't even know who was doing the instigating.

"One time I was late for class and had metal heel plates on my shoes," Chester reminisced. "Mrs. Williams said, 'Boy, don't you know you're late?'

"Meadow's in the back sayin', 'Tell her off, Chester.' I thought, *Oh, man, no!* But Meadow kept sayin', 'Tell her off,' and with my girlfriend sittin' there, I thought I had to say something.

"I said, 'Well, I'm late. So what?' She says, 'I'll tell you what you do. You go back out and come back in walkin' the way you're supposed to.'

"Again Meadow's back there sayin', 'Hey, I'd tell her I'm not gonna do anything!'

"I left and came back, walking the same loud way, and the next thing I knew I had to stay after school for a week. Do you remember that, Meadow?"

"No man, you're lying."

Or maybe Chester just has a better memory than I do.

12

Basketball? Football? Or Both?

You might assume that a typical Globetrotter goes to the right university, becomes a standout, and is discovered. That didn't happen with me.

I was so young and naive that I didn't know how it was going to happen. I just knew it was. I hung around Wilmington all summer after graduation, playing baseball and working out, shooting baskets whenever I could.

Almost every day my dad asked me what I was going to do. "I don't know, Dad. I'm hopin' I hear from the Globetrotters."

He'd shake his head. "Meadow, the Globetrotters don't even know you're alive. You know how bad I want you to get an education. Pick a school. Go. You'll never regret it. I'll be proud. You can play basketball at college."

I knew he was right, but I was stalling. The fact is, I was scared. I didn't want to go where the Trotters wouldn't be able to find me. And I wanted to play football just as much as I wanted to play basketball. Not for a career, of course, but for the fun and the competition. Until I was a Globetrotter, I didn't think I should rule out any sport I really enjoyed.

My father tried to reason with me. He had me help him on his route. I built up my arms by standing up on the Waste Paper and Recycling Company truck and lifting the cartons full of paper that he handed up, then dumping them and tossing the carton back down to him.

He stayed on my case, grunting with the effort of the work, but still talking a mile a minute. "Meadow, you got to decide. I don't want to see you in Wilmington the rest of your life when you can get out and do something with your life. You don't want to be like me."

He was right in one sense. I didn't want to stay in Wilmington. I was expected to excel. People thought I was somebody who would make it. I didn't want to be a gambler either, living from one paycheck to the next, hoping I wouldn't lose so much that I could hardly pay the rent. The way Dad gambled, he couldn't afford to gamble.

But I was in a mood to argue. "You've been a good dad. I wouldn't mind being like you."

You can't argue with a know-it-all high-school graduate. He'd just shake his head. "How many scholarship offers you got by now?"

I sighed. We'd been through it before. "Seventy for football. Sixty-something for basketball."

"How many for both?"

I shrugged. "Coach Corbin said another one came in yesterday. That makes about twenty for both."

"What are you gonna do? Where do you want to go?"

"I want to be a Globe—"

Now he was mad. "I *know* you want to be a Globetrotter! And I hope someday your dream comes true! But it ain't gonna happen with you sittin' around here all the time. Now if you had to choose a college, which would you choose?"

"I dunno."

"You gonna make me choose for you?"

I stared at him. "I guess I wouldn't mind goin' to college in Florida."

"Good! That's fine. You got a couple of offers from down there, don't you?"

I nodded.

"Florida A & M was one of 'em, right?"

I nodded again.

"Football or basketball?"

I shrugged.

"Both?"

"I don't know. Maybe. I think so," I admitted.

"Go there. Try it. It won't cost you nothin' but a train ticket, and I'll pay that. Meadow, make up your mind."

I was through talking about it. Whenever Dad brought it up again after that, I changed the subject. I knew it frustrated him, but it frustrated me, too. Not too many of my buddies were going off to college. Most of them were getting jobs they would have for decades. Getting settled. If I left Wilmington, I wanted it to be because I was going home. Home to my family. Home to the Globetrotters. We would travel all over the country and the world. I didn't know any of the Trotters, but they would be the big, black, happy, secure family I had never had.

I told Coach Corbin I didn't know what to do. I was leaning toward just waiting on the Globetrotters. He said he would write Abe Saperstein, the owner-coach, but that I should do what made me happy. "You know, a little college to fall back on wouldn't be bad, and it would make your daddy happy."

"That's for sure. But it wouldn't make me happy," I said.

"Well, you got to do what you got to do. I don't know about sittin' around waitin' for the Trotters, though, Meadows. I know it's been your lifelong dream, but it's a long shot. You have to know that."

I knew, but I didn't like to think about it, let alone talk about it. Coach Corbin, who was right nearly 100 percent of the time, was wrong about one thing. When he said I had to do what I had to do, he was underestimating Peanut Lemon. So was I. I knew Dad was determined that I have everything he never had, and I knew he wanted me to go to college, but I guess I didn't really know how committed he was to that.

In late August I was at the school yard. That morning we had lost a close baseball game. I had made an unassisted double play, fielded several chances cleanly, and struck out four times. Then we had played basketball in our sneakers and shorts and sleeveless shirts for two hours in the blazing sun. Now we sat playing cards, brushing the flies away, and sweating.

We talked low and slow, playing the dozens, chuckling. It was fun, but I was antsy. High-school football practice would be under way within a week. A week later school would start, and I would be left out. Out of high school, not in college, not a Trotter. Just waiting. It bothered me, but I wasn't saying so.

"That your dad, Lemon?"

I glanced over my shoulder. "His truck at least." The horn sounded. I kept looking. Dad waved me over. "Hi, Dad."

"Get in, Meadow. It's time for school."

"What you talkin' 'bout?"

He nodded toward the back. Two suitcases were packed. In his shirt pocket was my train ticket. "They're expecting you at Florida A & M. Playtime is over, son."

Somehow I knew there would be no more arguing about it. When my dad made up his mind, that was it. In fact, at first, I felt kind of relieved that the decision had been made for me.

Florida Agricultural & Mechanical University in Tallahassee seemed like a mistake from the minute I boarded the train. Dad wasn't one for outward shows of emotion, and though I'm sure the lump in his throat was as big as mine, he just busied himself helping with my luggage. Even when he was shaking my hand— his idea of a kiss and a hug, and an I-love-you-son, and an I'm-proud-of-you all wrapped into one—it was hard for him to look me in the eye.

I kept assuring him that I'd be all right, that I'd write, that I'd get back whenever I could. I would do my best and behave and remember everything he had told me, which was my way of saying, "I know, Dad. I know." His making the decision and dragging me off to the train station was as close as he could come to sending me off to school and paying for it. I loved him deeply in a way I couldn't express. "Hey, maybe with me gone, you and your lady can quit screamin' at each other all the time." He smiled, embarrassed.

The train rumbled through North Carolina, South Carolina, Georgia, and Florida, all in one long day. My general uneasiness with the situation turned to anger that I was leaving, frustration that I couldn't somehow just will myself to be a Globetrotter, and drop-dead fear of the unknown.

I didn't know what I was getting myself into. I didn't know anyone. My only hope was that I would room with someone who was an athlete and that I would fall in with the football and basketball players. The fact that there was a welcoming committee at the train station didn't help much. It wasn't for me, not that I expected it to be. It was for anyone heading for Florida A & M.

The kids helping newcomers were excited and bubbly, but I wasn't. I didn't know it yet, but I had never prepared myself to give A & M a chance. And because I had that attitude, the place wasn't going to win me over.

Before I knew it, I was in line, my luggage stashed somewhere. I had forms to fill out, keys to be assigned, and instructions to follow. When a man behind a desk compared all my forms with correspondence about me from a file, he told me what dorm I was in, how to sign up for classes, and that I should report to the athletic department two weeks before the first scheduled basketball workout. I would be on the freshman team.

"Uh-huh, thank you. And where do I report for football?"

"Pardon me?"

"Football. I'm supposed to be on the football team, too."

"You are?"

I nodded. "On scholarship."

"Let me check. I had you down for a full ride for the basketball scholarship. Generally if there are two sports, they split the scholarship."

"Well, it's supposed to be for both."

He checked and shook his head. "I'm sorry, Mr. Lemon. It could be our mistake. Did you talk with someone directly?"

"No, it was a letter." He showed me their copy of my letter. There was no mention of football. "Well, could I go out for football anyway?"

"I don't know anything about that. They've been practicing two weeks already. You could check with the coaches."

I headed for the gym. If I couldn't play football, I didn't even want to stay. The coaches were out at practice. The sun was high, the day humid. Everyone I talked to was the wrong guy. Finally, I was directed to the head football coach. I hardly knew what to say. I introduced myself, but he hardly took his eyes off the field. "What can I do for ya?"

"I want to come out for football."

"Too late, son. Walk-ons reported two weeks ago. Only a couple of 'em made it anyway."

"I was all-state in North Carolina three years. Receiver and deep back."

"Then why weren't you on scholarship?"

"I am. I mean I was. Or I thought I was."

"Which is it?"

"I'm on a basketball scholarship, and I thought I also had a football scholarship."

"Nah, we don't do it that way. We haven't had a basketball-football ride combination in years. Basketball coach thinks you pansies will get hurt out here."

"I'll take the risk."

He turned and looked me up and down, as if trying to judge me by sight. "Fast?"

"Good enough speed."

"Height?"

"Almost six one and growing."

"Weight?"

"Uh, 190."

"Yeah, sure, boy. If you're a pound over 170, I'll buy you a dinner. If not, you buy. Deal?"

I shook my head. "About 165, maybe a little more."

He pointed out two freshman receivers. Both were taller and heavier and faster than I was. The deep backs were rugged, too. "Lemon you said your name was?" I nodded. "I 'preciate your interest, you understand, but it wouldn't be fair to the other guys to let you come out now. And I've got to be honest with you. It wouldn't be fair to you either. The odds are against you makin' this team, and your basketball coach would make you choose between football and basketball. If you had to choose, what would you say?"

I hesitated. I know I looked like a basketball player to him. He nodded knowingly. I admitted it.

He looked back to the field but kept talking. "Like I say, son. Thanks for comin' out, but you stick with basketball, huh? And good luck."

"That's it? It's not up to me?"

"Not unless you're willing to give up your basketball scholarship and try out as a walk-on. Listen, I'm busy here, okay?"

I walked away. If I wasn't going to play football, what was I going to do? Basketball season seemed years away. I could have made some friends, but I was homesick. When classes started, school seemed boring. I called home.

Dad was glad to hear from me, and I pretended to be doing okay, all the while looking for a reason to leave. "Meadow, listen, I'll bet you're glad I sent you down there! Your draft notice came the other day."

"My draft notice?"

"Yeah! Into the army. But if you're enrolled in a college, you can get a deferral. Don't worry about it. I'll send it to you, and you have the school fill out all the stuff."

A plan was forming in my mind. If I couldn't be a Globetrotter and I couldn't play football and I couldn't wait for basketball season, I might as well be in the army. A couple of weeks later, I started packing.

When I got home, I went straight to see Coach Corbin. My dad would be so disappointed. Coach had been looking for me. "I got a telegram from A & M, Meadows. They're looking for you. They want me to send you back."

"I can't do it, coach. It's not for me." I didn't have the heart to tell him that I was going to be drafted into the army. He knew I could stay out if I wanted.

"But your education, your basketball scholarship. . . ." He sounded like my dad.

I just sat shaking my head. "All I want to be is a Globetrotter."

"You know they're playing in Raleigh in two weeks?"

I was stunned. "In person? I mean, the actual Globetrotters right there in Raleigh?" He nodded. "Oh, Coach, I'd give anything to see them."

"I'm sure they're sold out by now."

"Yeah, but you know Saperstein, right?"

"I've met him."

"And you wrote him about me?"

He nodded. "But I never heard back. He gets lots of letters from high-school coaches."

"Yeah, yeah, but I'll bet he'd at least get us into the field house for the game if you called him. Will you call him, Coach?"

Spike Corbin shook his head. But he reached for the phone. I could hardly believe he actually got through. "Abe, I'd just like to bring the kid I wrote you about to see the team. Any possibilities?"

He was smiling when he hung up. "He says all we have to do is introduce ourselves to Marques Haynes. Abe won't be there, but Haynes will get us in."

"*The* Marques Haynes? I'm gonna meet Marques Haynes?"

"Looks like it."

"And the other guys? Rookie Brown, Leon Hillard, Goose Tatum?"

"Good chance. You'll *see* 'em anyway. Now you'd better get home and tell your dad you're back."

"He'll kill me."

"He'll understand. . . . Oh, and Meadows, Abe said he'd have Marques look you over. If you show him anything, he'll give you a shot."

My eyes grew wide. "What does that mean?"

"I don't really know, but I'd take some trunks and be prepared to work out a little."

"Are you serious?"

"That's what I'd do, Meadows. Don't get your hopes up. You're just out of high school. But be prepared."

13

A Date in Raleigh

My dad slammed things around and gave me the silent treatment for a few days. What hurt the most was that he said he had no interest in coming with me to watch the Globetrotters. I knew he couldn't afford to take the time off anyway, but it would have made me feel a whole lot better if he'd just said he wished he could join me.

I had to respond to my draft notice with the admission that I wasn't enrolled in college, so my draft physical was in three weeks. Guess where? Raleigh. At least my decision to serve my country made Dad feel better about my future. That seemed a little more solid and predictable to him than basketball, even though I think he was getting used to the idea that I hadn't really been cut out for college. I suppose I would have been as nervous about joining the army—maybe more so—as going to college, except that I had something much more overwhelming to worry about. Meeting Marques Haynes.

I had no idea what to expect. I would take my shoes and socks and trunks and a top, but would he really have time to watch me work out? Is that what they wanted? How often did that happen? And what were the odds he would like what he saw? What would Marques tell me? Get some college basketball experience? Should I tell him I was going into the army?

The suspense drove me crazy. I worked out long and hard every day, bypassing questions about my short stay in Tallahassee by talking about getting to see the Globetrotters. I didn't tell anyone about Marques Haynes looking me over. What if that just meant that he would talk to me and see what I looked like, how big and all that. I was a shade under six one and hoped to grow at least another inch or two in two weeks!

I ran those questions over in my mind so much I got tired of talking to myself. I talked with Coach Corbin until he'd heard enough, too.

I could hear the irritated edge in his patient voice, though he spoke with love. He said, "Meadows, do this. Put all your questioning and your nervous tension into sharpening your game and increasing your stamina. For the sake of your hopes, assume you're just going to get an autograph from Marques Haynes and send greetings back to Abe through him. In the unlikely event that he has the time and the facility available to watch you work out a little, work on your game as if it was the opportunity of a lifetime."

"But what will he want to see? Slam dunks? Reverses? Fancy dribbling?"

"I don't know. Let him tell you. But remember, all that fancy stuff means nothing if you can't move, fake, dribble, pass, shoot, and rebound. Right?"

I nodded. And I worked. I doubt I ever whipped myself into such good shape in so short a time. I can't say I quit wondering and worrying, but I did follow Coach's advice. I hadn't played competitively since the basketball season the previous winter, but now I got into any game I could. I suppose I risked hurting myself and spoiling what slim chance I had, but sitting around just made me nervous.

If I hadn't been so exhausted at the end of each day, I couldn't have slept so soundly. But I was punishing my body so much that I drifted right off every night, dreaming of playing basketball the way no one ever thought possible. In my dreams I was impressing Marques Haynes with leaps that went up and floated down, shots that never missed, ballhandling that dazzled.

By the time there were just a few days before the trip, I had quit allowing myself to even think about the possibility of not getting to work out. Would it be before the game? After? Would I be the only one, or did they do this in every city with a dozen or two—or a hundred?

What if Abe's message never got to Haynes, and we didn't even get in? I couldn't think about it anymore.

Finally, the big day came. I was up early, shooting lazily. There was nothing more to do to get my body and my mind in shape. I felt like I could shoot over or through anyone on earth. As I recall it, a small carload of us headed north to Raleigh very early in the day. I believe Jukie Johnson drove, and Earl and Coach Corbin went along. Earl says Coach didn't ride with us, but about two dozen other people claim *they* did. If everybody went on that trip who thinks they did, we must have gone in a bus.

All I remember is that I was cramped in the back seat with my duffel bag, sweating and wondering if we would ever get there. The nightmare of nightmares hit me when we finally pulled to within sight of the field house. The parking lot was full. The crowd had spilled out of the doors. The ticket window was closed, with a Sold Out sign pasted over it.

We parked across the street and ran over. We heard people laughing and cheering inside. Had the game already started? I was sick! The closer we got, the more we could hear. People hoisted each other up to peek in the windows and over the transom. I knew the magic circle was in progress because I heard the strains of "Sweet Georgia Brown."

My friends strained to see and hear, wondering what we were going to do. I was a shy kid at that time, but nothing was going to get in the way of my seeing the Globetrotters. It was as if I had gotten to the Promised Land and found it surrounded by a twelve-foot wall. I would have sneaked in or crashed in or whatever I had to. I had been wanting to see the Globetrotters in person since I was eleven years old.

I spun in a circle, looking for a break in the crowd. Suddenly, from the back, here came a black man who looked familiar. Could it be? What was he doing out here? It was Marques Haynes! People were reaching out for him, thrusting paper and pencils in his face, but he was looking up, just trying to get in and join the team. He was the player-coach. He had to get in there. I noticed he was limping.

"Mr. Haynes, I'm Meadow Lemon. Mr. Saperstein was supposed to have written or called you. . . ."

Haynes had heard me. He turned and looked at me. "You're Lemon?" The sun stood still. The action went to slow motion. I didn't hear all the voices, shouting, pleading with Marques for an autograph. I didn't hear the music or the laughter or the applause from inside. I barely heard the crashing of my own heart. I opened my mouth. *Please, God, let words come out.* I nodded. He signaled that I should follow him.

I pointed to my companions. "My friends, uh, I. . . ."

He was talking. "Yeah, Abe called me. Said you'd be comin'. How you doin'?"

I was running to keep up as we brushed past the ticket taker and down the corridor to the locker room. "Mr. Haynes, can my friends, uh . . . ?"

He looked over his shoulder, slowing only slightly. "Oh, man, I'm sorry. I guess not. Man, Abe didn't say anything about anyone else. If it wasn't packed, you know. . . ."

I knew. But I felt bad for my friends. I didn't know what else I could say or do. I just hoped they'd understand.

Was this really happening? Was I actually walking toward a locker with a Globetrotter? Only in America. He pushed the door open. A couple of Trotters were on their way out. One called out to him, "Circle's goin', Marques!"

"I can hear that, man!"

"How's the knee? You playin'?"

"Nah. Not today. Goose out there?"

"Yeah. Just got here."

"Good. We'll be all right."

I couldn't think of anything to say. I stood stupefied. "Goose Tatum?" As if there was another Goose on the Trotters.

Haynes smiled and nodded. "Best in the business. He'll have the place rockin' this afternoon."

The big man was stripping down. He was an incredible specimen. Long, lanky, dark, powerful. I was proud. Of what, I didn't know, but I felt a kinship with him, and I knew I was being foolish.

When he got his shorts on, he padded over to a black trunk and pulled out a couple of uniform shirts. He held them up in front of him as if judging their size. *Surely he has his own jersey and regular number!* He draped a shirt on the edge of the trunk and pulled out a pair of shorts.

I have never gotten used to the shiny material Trotter uniforms are made of. It thrilled me just to see the material in color for the first time. I had imagined it after watching it on the screen in black and white, and if anything, this was more impressive than I could have imagined. Haynes tossed the uniform to me. "Got shorts and shoes?"

"Yeah."

"Suit up."

I stood there with the uniform draped on my arm, which had instinctively shot out to catch the clothes. "Suit up?"

"Hurry, boy." He was pulling his shirt on. He sat down to put on his shoes. From the gym came announcements and laughter, introductions. "You're from where? Wilmington?"

I nodded.

"And it's Lemon? Meadow Lemon?"

I nodded again, still not moving.

"Well, Meadow Lemon, we gonna kill two birds with one stone tonight. I'm gonna let you play some for me 'cause I need another day off this knee. And that'll give me a chance to do what Abe says, and that is to give you a look-see. That all right with you?"

"You mean in the game?"

Haynes quit pretending that he didn't know he had just dropped a bomb. He stood taller with his shoes laced up and squeaked over to me. He put a hand on my shoulder. "Look at it this way, boy. There's not much time for you to get nervous, and I don't have to stay after the game and find a practice gym. I know it's short notice, but if you've got something to show me, show me out there. Okay?"

I nodded.

"You can find your way?"

I nodded again.

And he left.

My fingers were stiff and numb. My ankle was sore from the cramped ride. I was sweating. My arm went through the neck hole first. I had to take the trunks off and put them on again to get them in the proper order. I tied one shoe and then had to untie it to tighten the laces all the way up. This wasn't happening. It was impossible. It was a dream.

Just getting to see the Trotters would have been more than enough. I'd have paid. To meet Marques Haynes, that was bonus. If he'd invited me to sit on the bench, I'd have been in glory. To wear a uniform stunned me. To play, unreal. I thought I was going to throw up.

I turned to run from the locker room, but I was so excited I couldn't make the turn at that speed and bumped into the wall, then the door, which swung wide and banged against the wall, a booming echo ricocheting down the hall. A security guard looked up from his paper to see a skinny black kid in a baggy Harlem Globetrotter uniform bounding down the hall, heading for the gym.

I fought through a small crowd, which quickly parted. "It's a player! It's a Globetrotter!"

As I entered the gym, Marques pointed at the announcer, who read from a little slip. "For the first time in a Globetrotter uniform, the Trotters present Meadow Lemon, from our own Wilmington, North Carolina."

The crowd erupted. The applause and cheering were sounds I'd never forget. Over twenty-five years later, I can still say that I received a greater ovation from those homestate folks that day than any of my entire career.

14

Uncle Sam and Cripple Creek June

I ran over to the bench and sat down on the far end. As the game began, I followed the lead of the guys on the bench. Once the gags and routines got under way, they all stood and gathered around like interested observers. They laughed and poked each other and joined in the cavorting.

At first just being there, fooling around with the guys on the side, was enough for me. I was living a dream, and I knew it. That in itself was a miracle! But by the time the half was over, and Marques Haynes still hadn't put me in the game, I was beginning to wonder. Had he changed his mind and decided to wait until after the game to watch me work out?

Finally, near the end of the third quarter, when the Globetrotters had built a huge lead, Marques put me in. It all happened so fast I could hardly comprehend it. I was there with my idols, passing to Rookie Brown and Goose Tatum and Jumping Johnny Williams. Boy, could he fly!

They put me in a corner where I wouldn't have to handle the ball much. I was told to stay out of the way when they were doing tricks and routines and just play by instinct. "If you get the ball and you're open, take a shot. Otherwise, keep it moving. We never slow down. Play tough D and go for the steal and the rebound all you want. Watch, but stay involved."

As we ran to our positions, Rookie Brown said, "Just stay behind me and do what I do." It sounded like good advice until I realized he was five inches taller than I was and couldn't jump very well. He could barely stuff the ball.

I ran up and down the court, watching, listening, wondering. I was in a daze. Maybe it was just for a few minutes, but I was a Globetrotter. Just like that. I came to try out, and I was getting to play at the same time.

I mostly tried to stay out of the way of the hardest passes I'd ever seen. That ball could have taken my head off! I had to watch the arms of the man with the ball, because I might not see the ball once he let it loose. A couple of times, a pass came to me. I made sure I fired it right back to the one who passed it. That seemed to be one of their techniques. Pass on the run, and get the ball back as you go. Always set up the other guy's shot, not your own.

I was afraid that any minute, Marques would take me out of the game. It wasn't fair to the other subs to let a newcomer take their playing time. But during one break he told me that as long as I was productive, I could stay in. Up to then, I didn't think I had been productive at all. Still, I hadn't gotten in anybody's way. It would have been easy to mess up everything, thrown into a situation like that.

I reminded myself that this was what I had dreamed of most of my life and prepared myself for since I had come back from Florida. I had good skills. I believed in myself. It was time to quit standing around with my mouth hanging open and show these guys that I belonged.

The next time the ball came to me, I faked a pass on the run, drove the base line, and scored on a reverse lay-up. Rookie Brown tried to top that with a stuff, but I followed with a twisting fly through the lane, followed by a resounding reverse jam. The applause, just like when I had been introduced, surged through me, and I was hooked. I would have done anything to get those people to roar their approval.

I was careful to watch Haynes on the bench and the other stars to see how they reacted. Everyone nodded and smiled, so I kept it up. I was skying on my jump shot, grabbing rebounds, stealing the ball, feeding the fast break, following it up with slam dunks, and doing something I had rarely done during a basketball game. Smiling.

During the game I heard something strange. Teammates called Rookie Brown, William. Captain Babe Pressley they called Louis.

They called Goose, Reece. These guys had real names! I wondered if I would get a nickname if I made the team.

The buzzer sounded to indicate the end of the third quarter. I looked over at Marques, but he didn't motion me off the court. We ran off the court and sat on the bench while Marques discussed strategy. Then the final quarter began.

About halfway through, Marques sent a sub in to relieve me. I'd played for the equivalent of a full quarter. Marques must have thought I'd contributed something.

After the game was over, I listened carefully in the locker room for signals about how my game had gone. I got a lot of compliments, and Johnny Williams told me that he and I could really put on a show.

I pinched myself to see if this was real. I showered and dressed in a daze.

The Trotters weren't big on keeping records back then, and I don't recall the final score. They beat almost everybody and ran the scores up as much as they felt they needed to. Everyone scored a lot, some on gag plays that really shouldn't have counted.

I had fun, but I wasn't into any of the funny stuff. I dunked and did whatever else I could to get the ball to the hoop. I scored about 12 points.

All the nervous tension I had been storing over the prospect of just seeing and meeting these guys had been poured into my performance. I felt I played even better than I had in the Shaw University game and the last regular game of my high-school career. After all, this game had been at the professional level with the best players in the world.

Goose Tatum drew me aside before he left. "You're a good-lookin' ballplayer, Lemon. Did you enjoy it?"

"You bet! And you were hilarious, Goose." I told him about my bag with his name on the side, and how much I enjoyed his act and his talent.

"I appreciate that, kid, and a couple of times watchin' you I thought I was lookin' in the mirror, no kiddin'. I thought, *Here I am on the bench, and there I am on the floor.* But listen to me. It's my job, and there's not much future in it. You know what's good for you, you forget this and go to college, hear?"

I shook my head. "I don't know. This is what I've always wanted to do."

"You can't make a living doing this. Take it from me."

I didn't buy a word of it. I found out later that both Tatum and Haynes were making around twenty-five thousand a year at that time. Pretty good money in the early fifties. The lowest paid player on the leading Trotter team got seven hundred and fifty a month. That would have made me feel like a millionaire.

Tatum was a true classic, the clown who brought humor to the basketball court. Before him, black baseball teams had a corner on comedy, and no one could figure out how to transfer it to basketball. Goose did it with the magic circle, stealing a page from baseball's book on playing pepper. I knew I had been in the presence of a legend.

You hear people talk about walking on air. I wish I could think of a new way to say it. I was so high I didn't know if I'd ever come down. I should have been exhausted. In a way I was drained, but I couldn't have slept if you paid me. Marques complimented me on my game. "You've got the fundamentals and the flash. The comedy will come with time. I'm gonna tell Abe just what you showed today. You take care now."

Just like that, it was over. In one way I felt part of that team. And yet they were gone. Some of them were older than I had expected. All looked tired. But they were together. They were playing basketball. They headed one way down the hall to their bus, and I headed the other way to my friends.

Had they ever gotten in? Did they miss it? Would they believe me? I found out soon enough. All the way home I couldn't get a word in. They kept talking over each other, interrupting, claiming they knew, they *always* knew, I would make it. The game had been announced outside by loudspeaker, so they had kept track of my playing.

Earl was ecstatic. "Meadow, you know that center, Neals Anderson, you scored over?"

I nodded.

"Well, he's six ten and was a star at the university. When you kept scoring over him, not around him but over him, that's when I knew you had it made. Did they sign you?"

I couldn't explain. Jukie was carrying on about how he used to be better than I was but how I had passed him up, just like he always knew I would. Coach Corbin knew I would be great some-day, too. He went on and on about my dedication. I had never felt better in my life.

After celebrating, we got home late that night. I wasn't tired. I glowed. Dad was home alone. I asked where his woman was. "Who knows? She started screamin', and I told her to get lost. She'll be back. She's never gone long."

I told him about my dream come true. He sat in the darkness, a light from the street streaking across his cheek. I could see him slowly shaking his head, I hoped from awe rather than disgust. When he spoke, it was just above a whisper. He said, "My boy done that? My own boy, Meadow? You worked hard for it, son. Didn't I always tell you that? That if you worked hard enough for somethin', it would pay off? Didn't I?"

I wanted to rush to him, to hug him. But that wasn't how we communicated. "That's what you always told me, Dad. But I don't think you thought I was gonna do it with a basketball."

He stared at me. I could hardly hear him. "No, that's true. At first I didn't. But you wanted it so bad, worked for it so hard. Now I wish I coulda been there."

"You were working. I understand."

He looked at the floor. "Yeah, but I shoulda been there. I coulda made it."

"It's all right. Dad. You'll get plenty of chances to see me. Mr. Haynes told me that if Abe likes what he hears, I'll get called to tryouts in Chicago at the end of their season. I didn't tell him I'd be in the army."

"Maybe you can get leave."

"Maybe."

"Did you say Chicago?"

"Yeah, that surprised me, too, Dad. I always thought the Globetrotters were from Harlem. They're from Chicago."

He stood slowly and made his way past me toward the stairs. "Peanut Lemon's kid is actually gonna be a Globetrotter. Who'd ever believe it? Wait till your Aunt Maggie hears about this. And your mom. You know, you'll be the first Lemon boy in years who's really been able to get outta here. When you came home from Florida, I thought you were gonna be stuck here. But now it's the army, and then the Globetrotters."

He fell just short of telling me how proud he was. But I knew.

Being inducted into the army was better than attending Florida A & M, but it was a lot worse than joining the Globetrotters. The racial unfairness saddened me. We had been sworn in together, blacks and whites, but when we stopped to eat on the way to the post, blacks ate one place, whites another. We stayed overnight in a tenth-rate hotel and paid for our breakfast with little coupons.

Luckily, I was in shape for basic training at Fort Jackson, South Carolina, just outside Columbia. Sixteen weeks of hard labor was more like it. I thought every officer and drill sergeant hated us, but they were just doing what they had to do to get us in shape for combat in Korea if necessary.

I had signed up for two years, but I left with Coach Corbin, Dad, and Earl all the information about how to reach me when I heard from the Globetrotters. When a few weeks passed and I realized I couldn't walk away from this the way I had college, I felt trapped.

Fortunately, depending on how you look at it, I ran into a black guy who called himself Cripple Creek June. He was a bad dude. Carried a switchblade and was a dice player. Watching him roll dice convinced me I never wanted to start. He could make those dice talk, and the more uneven the surface, the better. I saw him roll six sevens in a row on his bunk! He did teach me poker, though. How to cheat, how to recognize a cheat, who to cheat, and who not to cheat. I used the knowledge later, but just for fun.

He liked to brag about all the people he had suckered or cut up back in his hometown of Cripple Creek, South Carolina. Most of us believed him, and I decided to get on his good side. I didn't want trouble from him or anyone else, so I figured it was better to be his buddy than not. Funny thing, for all his big talk, he came out with a good line once in a while. I grumbled one day about the unfairness of the way we blacks were treated. Cripple Creek grinned and said, "Look at it this way. A hundred years ago it was the Indians they were fighting. Give 'em another hundred years. They'll come around."

There was a public outcry about the number of blacks being killed in Korea at that time, so the army cut back on the number they sent over. That was good news for me, but I was still infuriated by what I believed to be prejudice on the part of the military for letting the problem get out of hand in the first place. An awful lot of blacks from the South, especially from my unit at Fort Jackson, had been among the first to die over there. Delaying my induction by going to college for a few weeks might have saved my life.

Cripple Creek June was an interesting and fun guy to be around, but I still hated the army. It was grueling, hot, filthy, and demeaning. On the rifle range we had an exercise where you had to crawl on your belly through the mud and avoid live ammunition flying a foot over your head. A young white kid from Arkansas crawling just ahead of me suddenly froze, and I heard him groan a four-letter word.

I was frustrated. "Keep movin', man!" If we didn't get across the field in time, they declared us dead, and we had to do it again. I thought about climbing over him, but I couldn't stay low enough. Slowly, I worked around him.

I got to the end and ran over to the sergeant. "Sir, a man is still on the range."

"I can see that, Lemon! You think I'm blind?"

"He seems to have panicked, sir."

"Well, why don't you stroll out and have a chat with him then, Lemon? Maybe counsel him? Is that what you want to do?"

"No, sir. I just wanted to inform you, sir."

He dripped with sarcasm before he exploded, "Thank you, Lemon. NOW GET BACK WITH YOUR UNIT!"

I hated that place. I ran to get into position. We stood at attention, oozing slime as the sergeant swaggered between the wire mesh to get to the whimpering recruit. "Get up, son!" The man was still paralyzed. "I SAID GET UP, BOY!" The man stirred but didn't really move. "SEND ME TWO VOLUNTEERS TO GET THIS BOY ON HIS FEET!"

Two buddies of mine were sent. They put a hand under each arm and pulled him from the mud. Dangling from a fist clenched so tight his knuckles were white was a four-foot rattlesnake about three inches in diameter. The young man had stayed down, stayed cool, grabbed that rattler, and squeezed the life out of it.

The sergeant pried the man's fingers from the snake, and it flopped to the mud. The sergeant saluted. I wanted out of that place in a bad way.

A few days later, on my belly on the rifle range taking some target practice with an M-1, I got soaked. A cold rain had fallen the night before, and a cloudy day kept the sun from drying anything. I was miserable. A chill took hold of me. By the next morning, I was wheezing.

I was put in the infirmary, but I've never been terribly fond of needles. Every time I turned around, and sometimes when I didn't, somebody wanted to insert a sharp object into my hide. I got well real quick, though I heard them talking about pneumonia. I think I flat talked myself out of it.

Still weak, I had to act normal, or I'd be sent straight back in. In the army, either you're too sick to carry on your duties, which requires admission to the infirmary and turns loose the needle brigade, or you're well enough to do everything you were assigned.

I was assigned back to the rifle range to finish my M-1 practice. But by now the sun had baked the mud into hard knobs that cut into my body no matter how I positioned myself. I'm basically an optimist, but basic training will change anyone. I was working on a real hate. I wanted a home even if it was a bus that traveled hundreds of miles day and night.

I had stayed with my aunt, then my dad, then my mom. I was an only child. I didn't want to stay in Wilmington all my life, but right now that looked pretty inviting. I knew it would be temporary. If only I could get out of Fort Jackson, South Carolina.

"Lemon!"

It was a private with a message. "Telegram for you at headquarters."

I was glad for any opportunity to get off that firing range. But a few moments later, I read a message I wish had never come:

DEEPLY REGRET TO INFORM YOU OF YOUR FATHER'S UNTIMELY PASSING DUE TO ACCIDENTAL KNIFE WOUND (STOP) RETURN HOME SOONEST (STOP).

15

Standing in the Back of the Bus— and the World

I phoned Wilmington to learn that the "accidental" knife wound was inflicted by Dad's common-law wife. Rage nearly overtook grief. Within an hour I was on a bus for the eight-hour ride home.

I felt like I was walking through a fog. I barely noticed the sea of white faces in the front half of the bus or the black faces at the back, demurely staring at the floor or out the window. There were no seats available in the back. Four were open in the front, but I had to stand in the back until a black got off.

Sadness, grief, rage, frustration screamed within me. I was an all-state high-school athlete, probably one of the youngest ever to play with the Harlem Globetrotters, had received over a hundred college scholarship offers in two sports, and was serving my country in the military. Now my father had been murdered, and on my trip home from the army—for the first hour anyway—I had to *stand*, let alone sit, in the back of the bus.

My world had caved in. My mother had long since remarried a handsome man (he would eventually die of alcoholism). My aunt had moved away. I was temporarily employed by Uncle Sam. I had no home. I was alone. And I wanted revenge. I don't know how many times I thought about getting off that bus, thumbing a ride back to Fort Jackson, breaking down my M-1, and taking it home with me. If I had, I'd have killed that woman. I know I would.

For some reason, I couldn't cry. Every time the bus lurched and jumped, I had to hold tighter to the rail above my head. When we finally changed buses, I got to sit alone for several miles. Then the tears came. I wanted to sob, but I didn't want anyone to notice. I buried my face in my shoulder. That way I looked like I was staring out the window. I was on my own, and the tears wouldn't stop. An elderly woman boarded at the next depot and shared the seat with me. She tried to make small talk. I couldn't even turn to speak to her.

In a daze, I arrived in Wilmington and was driven to the funeral home. Dad looked so strange dressed up in a suit. His face was lighter, his features compressed. I hurt so bad I couldn't respond. I was left alone with him, and I wanted to cry. I just couldn't. Pressure was building in me, but it was more anger than grief. I was mad. I wanted to see his woman. Several counseled me not to. I kept insisting.

Finally, I was told that she was in the hospital. "Good! Did Dad hurt her?"

"No, she's really upset over what happened."

"Well, I should think she would be! So am I! Where is she?"

"Meadow, she's lost her mind over this. She may never be the same."

"Me either, but I'll feel better if I can see her and tell her what she's done."

I was talked out of it. They were right. She never was the same. I'll never know exactly what happened, but I know it was ugly. There would have been nothing gained by my confronting her, and certainly not by trying to avenge Dad's death. At the funeral I was calm and, in a sense, peaceful. I couldn't cry, yet I felt such an emptiness that I didn't think it would ever be filled. People find it hard to believe, but I honestly feel that I mourned my father for more than ten years.

I know that sounds unnatural, but he was all I had. He was my anchor. I loved my mother, of course, but she had her own life, her own home, her own husband. I was eighteen years old and alone in the world.

My age came into play, too. Friends counseled me to check with Dad's employers to find out what kind of death benefits he had. They were meager, but they would have paid for putting him in the ground and paying off his debts. The story from the personnel manager was the worst. "I'm sorry, but these benefits are payable only to a surviving spouse or offspring of at least twenty-one years of age."

"So I get them in three years?"

"No, they must be claimed within twelve months of the death."

"I'm old enough for the army and to die for my country, but I'm not old enough to collect my dad's life insurance?"

"I'm sorry, son. It's not my decision."

A lawyer might have been able to help me get the money, but I didn't know anything about that. All I knew was that it would take my army paycheck for the next two years just to bury my dad. Fortunately, the army and the American Red Cross took care of it for me. I was grateful, but no less angry.

I still had ten weeks of basic training to finish before being shipped out—to where I didn't know yet—so I returned to Fort Jackson an angry, frustrated teen-ager. I had told a few people about having played a game with the Globetrotters and that my dream was to play with them someday, but no one believed it.

I was quicker than ever on the trigger, so if anyone crossed me, they regretted it. I just hoped I wouldn't get myself into trouble with the military police before I pulled myself together. The only outlet I had was sports, so a friend and I hung around the football field, hoping to get a chance to play. We were accused of trying to get out of work and duty, so we didn't make the team.

What I really wanted to do was to play basketball during my free time. That would be the only thing that could take my mind off the loss of my dad. The trouble was, there were already two blacks on the basketball team, and they didn't want any more. One was a lieutenant who had played the year before, so he had priority. The other was a great track man, the best on the post, so they didn't want to offend him by replacing him with me. Finally, they said I could practice against them. That was one thing the post was always short of, enough people to field two teams for a practice game.

I wanted to play. I wanted to start, but practicing would be okay. I could say enough by the way I played to vent a lot of anger and frustration. Those guys didn't know it, but they were going to suffer for the injustices I felt.

Didn't want me on their team, huh? Had enough blacks, huh? Didn't believe my Globetrotter story, huh? In all fairness, they didn't claim to be good players. They were just your average ex-high-school subs who enjoyed the game.

I showed up for practice. They put their starting five on the floor and aligned me with four guys who were just hanging around to watch. I jumped for our side and batted the tip to a teammate. He fumbled it to the other team, but I stole it back. I passed upcourt, but a teammate dropped it out of bounds. When the starters brought the ball up, I stole it, knew there was no one to pass to, and drove the lane. They filled it up, so I jumped, spun, and shot. Two.

For ten minutes, all I did was steal the ball, keep it, dribble the length of the floor, and score. I suppose it was unfair. They had, in essence, a Globetrotter to play against. I just wanted to make a statement, to take out my aggression on something or someone without causing any real pain. In the end, they just shook their heads. "We get the point, Lemon! All we're getting is practice in good sportsmanship. Lighten up a little, huh?"

After having been a happy-go-lucky kid with a ready smile and a sunny disposition, I was quickly becoming sullen and cynical. It wasn't me. I didn't want to be that way. But Dad had died, I felt like I was in prison, and I had myself convinced that the Globetrotters had forgotten about me.

I didn't hear a word from them, and that, of course, made me wonder if Marques Haynes had ever passed along his scouting report to Abe Saperstein. Assuming he hadn't, I decided I knew why. They were jealous, threatened. They didn't want to lose their jobs. I based my logic on a false premise and a lot of hurt, but I sure built a good case.

Finally, my military assignment came. I got a few days' leave to go home—to what? Then I took a train to New Jersey where I boarded a troop ship for a thirteen-day cruise to Italy. From there we took a train to Camp Roder at Headquarters Tactical Command, Salzburg, Austria.

If there was a bright spot in my military career, it was in Salzburg, seventy-five miles southeast of Munich, West Germany. That post wanted to have the best sports teams in the army in the three major sports. I played baseball, football, and basketball. Word had gotten around that I fancied myself a Globetrotter, so I quit talking about it.

The general, a typical stuffed-shirt type, approached me one day. "So, you played with the Harlem Globetrotters, eh, Lemon?"

"Yes, sir."

"You know no one around here believes that, don't you, son?"

"I got that impression, yes, sir."

"Well, I'll tell you what. I'm a basketball fan, and I'll be able to tell by watching you play whether there's any truth to it. For now, I'll give you the benefit of the doubt. For your sake, I hope you're telling the truth."

I didn't know what he was planning to do to me if I was lying—or if he thought I was lying. I was eager to show off a little. When I got to the basketball court, a bunch of guys had already chosen up sides, but there were only nine. I was assigned to the team that was short a player, and then I found out that the five we were playing were the starters for the camp team.

At least I can check out my competition for a starting job, I thought. The team was staring at me as we warmed up. I heard snickering and the word *Globetrotter,* then laughter. I enjoyed pressure, but they had more than pressure in mind. With the opening tip, I was hammered to the court with a hip. This was just a pickup game, so there was no ref to call it. I heard more laughter as I struggled to my feet and fought to catch my breath.

The opposing team scored and headed back my way. The man who had given me the hip ran past me. I yelled at him, "Hey, watch that next time!"

He glared at me, let me pass him up, and then ran up my back, pretending to go for the ball. I turned and swung wildly, catching him in the temple. He gasped and started to go down. Something snapped in me. Suddenly, he was my dad's murderer, he was the army, he was the white folk in the front of the bus, he was whatever had torn my mom and dad apart.

I hit him harder than I've ever hit anyone, and I kept swinging.

He rolled and crawled to get away. From the corner of my eye I saw two others coming toward me. I skipped out of bounds and grabbed a folding chair. I swung it around and around over my head, daring anyone to come close. "I don't want any trouble! I'm gonna be here for sixteen months, and I wanna play a little basketball! But I'm not gonna be walked on!"

I stormed out, no one having been really hurt. The next night, when I showed up again, there was a crowd. The confrontation had swept the post, and people wanted to see this crazy black boy who claimed to have played with the Globetrotters but who didn't have any self-control. They wondered if I could play basketball the way I fought.

I'll tell you one thing, nobody messed with me that night. And everybody, the general included, found out I could play basketball. I'm not proud of having been the best player in an army post. Those guys weren't there for their athletic ability. But it was fun showing off and flying through everyone to the basket.

Needless to say, I made the starting team for the camp, and we set about playing in tournaments. Our coach was a first sergeant who didn't really know the game. He took most of my whispered suggestions, and we started winning. After thirteen games we were nine and four. I was averaging 55 points a game, and my teammates averaged a total of 13.

I enjoyed getting so much shooting practice, but I kept worrying whether anyone else was having any fun. They assured me they were. "It's fun to be winning for a change, Lemon. Just keep it up."

It was strange. We would come up the court, then they would pass to me and stand around watching. If I passed to anyone, they passed right back to me like the ball was a hot potato. The only time anyone else scored was when I was taking a breather. I was the only defensive player, too, and there's nothing that will take it out of you quicker than rebounding all night.

I'd grab a rebound, flip it to someone, and then head up court, knowing the ball would come back to me and I'd be expected—by both teams—to shoot. The opposition double- and triple-teamed me all the time. At least that made it a challenge.

The games we lost were when I was so tired or so overplayed

that I was held to 40 or fewer points. One night as we walked to the court I heard an opposing player say, "Let Lemon have his 40, and we can win this."

I scored 75 in the first three quarters, and we led 83–81. I was so tired I could hardly move, so I suggested we stall. By freezing the ball for most of the fourth quarter, we won by 1. I scored 80 points. When we got to the locker room, I grabbed a small wood stool and limped to the showers. I turned the water on as hot as I could stand it, sat on that stool, and lobstered myself for about an hour.

Occasionally, humorous incidents spiced up the games. My favorite was the night I saw the general and his wife in the stands and I decided to show off. I had a plan for the first fast break I would get. Early in the second quarter, my chance came. I swiped at the ball as I came upcourt behind the opposing guard. That made him rush a pass, which bounced off his teammate and downcourt, past me. All I had to do, with no one around, was catch up to the ball, dribble once or twice, and take any unmolested shot I wanted.

I raced after the ball, dribbled it in flight, palmed it with my right hand, took off from the free-throw line, and jammed it through. The ball slammed off the floor so hard it went back up through the basket, something I hadn't planned. I caught it as it came back down through.

Everybody in the place was screaming. The general leaped to his feet, not realizing his wife had just done the same. He pumped his fists in the air, and his arm clobbered his wife, sending her sprawling two rows down the bleachers. Several enlisted men nearby rushed to her aid, trying to keep straight faces. When she got back up next to her husband, she took a swing at him!

In the next months, hundreds of enlisted men dreamed of that slap every time they became frustrated with the army and their commanders.

16

The Ship That Finally Came In

The only small consolation I had in the army was that I made some good friends. At that time I was running around with a guy named Toby, a great sparring partner who we all thought could have become a pro boxer. One day the letter I had waited for so long finally arrived. I couldn't wait to tell him about it.

Dear Private Lemon:
I'm sorry it has taken so long to get back to you. I received an excellent report on your game in Raleigh from our former coach Marques Haynes. You may have heard that he has left us to form a similar team. Congratulations on a great game and for being such an outstanding player.
    We will be playing in Vienna next month. If it would be convenient for you to get there, I would enjoy meeting you. A brochure is enclosed, telling exactly where and when we will be there. Hope you can make it, but I will understand either way.
Cordially,
Abe Saperstein
Harlem Globetrotters, Inc.
P.S. I was saddened to hear of the passing of your father.

I knew the army would let me go, with the way the general liked me. He was one tough, mean guy, but he liked his Globetrotter. When I showed the note to the general, it was as good as done. "I was the only one around here who wasn't skeptical, wasn't I, Lemon? Huh? Didn't I tell you I believed you all along? Yes, sir. The Harlem Globetrotters."

I smiled.

"So, son, will you be playing with them up there in Vienna? Shall I come?"

"Oh, no sir. I mean, I might, but he doesn't say that here, and I'd hate to have you come all that way and then me not play."

The truth was I was hoping and praying Abe would suit me up. If I was as good as Haynes had said, surely the boss man would want to get a look at me. I took my gear, just in case.

Toby went with me. What a trip! It was two hundred miles by train, and the butterflies in my gut increased with every mile.

I had seen Abe Saperstein in the movie *The Harlem Globetrotters,* but I was not really prepared for him. He was a little roly-poly white man in a brown sharkskin suit. I would discover later that it was one of two (the other was black) that made up his wardrobe. He pumped my hand and told me that in this game, I would get a true look at what it was like to travel with a barnstorming, international comedy basketball team. He gave me a uniform and sent me to Sweetwater Clifton's hotel room to change.

I hadn't met Sweetwater Clifton before. He was huge, about six eight and 265. He was probably one of the strongest athletes ever. Nobody messed with him, in spite of his high-pitched voice and his habit of calling everybody Honey. He was all man. If you ran into Sweet during a melee on the basketball court, you said excuse me and kept going.

That night he got me hooked on expensive French colognes. "Why don't you slap some of this on, Honey? It'll make you smell good." I loved it, started buying my own, and I still buy the same two brands to this day. A clerk recently told me I was using women's cologne. I told her I wasn't about to change now!

The Globetrotters in Vienna were a slightly different team than the one I had played with the first time. I had to get acquainted all over again. Goose wasn't with them. Neither was Rookie Brown. They had some impressive players, but I missed some of the stars I had met before.

The game was played outdoors on a portable floor, and it was all we could do to keep our feet and entertain the crowd, not to mention play impressively and win. Still, Abe saw what he hoped to see in me because later in his hotel room, he surprised me again.

"A year from now, we'll be back here for a thirty-day tour with about forty games."

"Forty games?"

He nodded. "We play several double-headers. If you can get your thirty-day leave to fit with our schedule, we'll put you on the payroll for a month." He didn't have to ask twice.

Toby and I were too late to catch a train back to Salzburg that night, and we hadn't arranged for a room. That didn't bother us. I was going to be a Globetrotter for thirty days! Even if it was a year away, that called for a celebration. We did the town.

When we finally got back to camp late the next day, we were dead tired. Everybody wanted to hear about the game and about my future, and I was only too happy to tell them. If only I could have told Dad. My life went from the depths to the heights with one letter from Abe Saperstein. On the one hand, it was what I had wanted all my life. On the other, I still had trouble believing it was happening.

The next summer I joined the Globetrotters in Karlsruhe, West Germany. The general had business in that area, and he invited me to go on his plane. We were late, and I hurried into the auditorium in my dress uniform, shoes gleaming. Most of the guys I had met in Raleigh and missed in Vienna were on this team, and they treated me like a long lost son. I grinned from ear to ear.

Goose Tatum shocked me by remembering who I was. "Look at ol' Meadow! He made it after all!" The guys surrounded me, and I shook hands with each. *This* was the feeling I wanted. They told me to hurry up and get into uniform, and just like in Raleigh, I was dressing to the tune of "Sweet Georgia Brown."

We traveled through Germany, France, Belgium, and Italy. It was just what I had dreamed it would be. Guys working together, playing together, living together, traveling together, enjoying each other. I earned two hundred dollars plus meal money, most of which I saved. By the time I got back to Salzburg, I was loaded with money and stories. I think some of the stories may have gotten better each time I told them, but the fun part was saying, meaning, and feeling that I was truly a Globetrotter now. I would find out later that it wasn't that easy, but for then, I was in.

Throughout the rest of my time overseas, I had a ball. Staying away from alcohol allowed me to stay out of trouble. I learned to drive, got in the motor pool, and was unofficial coach of several teams. I wasn't a commissioned officer, so someone else had to have the coaching title, but I secretly delivered the strategy.

By the end, I was refereeing basketball games to earn extra money, saving my paycheck, and drawing a small stipend from the Trotters for playing on the thirty-day tour and several subsequent weekend deals. I was making some money, having a good time, and I was in with the general. You can't get much more comfortable than that.

Once, when I had returned late from a set of weekend Globetrotter games, I slept in. An hour after everyone else was up and gone, the general came in for an inspection and demanded to know who was still in bed. I cringed, dreading what was to come. I'd seen men oversleep, and they lived to regret it. I pretended to still be asleep, all the while praying for a miracle. I got one.

"That's Lemon, sir. He had a Globetrotter game last night."

"Oh, well, then. Shh!"

I did the best I could in the army, once I decided not to run from it. I'm proud to say I served my country in some small way. But my heart wasn't in it. My heart was with the Globetrotters. I wanted to be with them for good.

When I finally got out of the service, I was shipped out of Italy onboard ship. We traveled through storm after storm, and I was sick almost the whole way home. I was miserable. One guy told me not to worry because no one ever died from seasickness. I told him, "It's the hope of dyin' that's keepin' me alive."

In Wilmington, everything seemed to have changed, even though I'd been gone a little less than two years. I felt lost. I couldn't find a job anywhere, and I was willing to do anything. I knew that someday soon I'd be leaving there and making a name for myself with the Globetrotters, but meanwhile, a man had to eat. I drew unemployment, which was twenty-one dollars a week for twenty-one weeks.

Now that I had played with the Globetrotters in Europe, I got up enough nerve to ask out a local girl named Angela. Angie knew she was a good looker. She had fair skin, wore her hair in a pony-tail, and had a round, cherub face. All that, and the talent to play the piano for the glee club, too. I was impressed.

In the course of our conversations, she mentioned that one of her best friends was a girl named Willye Maultsby. My throat went dry. "No kidding." I had forgotten that by now, little Willye Maultsby—the girl with the gorgeous natural beauty, the perfect complexion, the skin color that looked like she had a year-round tan—would be a grown-up, high-school senior.

Angela and I had talked about going to a movie one Friday night, but I had been unable to reach her to confirm it. Who should I run into at the grocery store that Friday morning but Willye? She remembered me as a friend of her sister Ophelia, and her smile lit up the place. She had indeed grown up. I tried to act cool, asking her if she might be seeing Angela that day. "If you do, would you mind asking her to meet me at the Ritz tonight at seven?"

I never heard whether Angela got the message, so I wasn't sure what to expect when I got to the theater. I was prepared to watch the movie alone, and I hoped Angela wouldn't be too upset that we hadn't connected. I hung around outside until almost time for the picture to start and up walked Willye. "I, uh, couldn't get a hold of Angela, and I, um, didn't want you to have to be here all by yourself."

Yeah, uh-huh. Pretty crafty. I was impressed. And that little maneuver told me volumes. The girl of my dreams had grown up. I hardly thought of Angela again, and I never asked Willye whether she admitted to her friend what she had done. Within a few months, it was irrelevant. Willye had graduated from high school, and we were in love.

We spent every available moment together. Often she just sat and watched me work out at the Boys' Club. That may have given me the false impression that she simply idolized me and didn't care what I did as long as we were together. That was the way I felt about her. I couldn't take my eyes off her, and I was always proud to be seen with her.

She was almost as pleased as I was when Abe Saperstein finally called and asked me to join the Kansas City All-Stars, one of the three opposition teams that travels with the Globetrotters and alternates playing against them.

If I'd given myself time to think about it, I might not have liked that idea. But I would be employed by the Globetrotters, and I had to start somewhere. Four hundred dollars a month was a whole lot better than twenty-one dollars a week. I couldn't show off and do my thing, but I would do everything I could to look like a model employee to management.

Pop Gates coached the All-Stars. He was tough, but all the guys loved him. I was assigned to room with Carl Green from New York City, a former star for a college in Winston-Salem, North Carolina.

There were only two months left in the Globetrotter season when I joined, but Carl and I grew to be good friends. We learned that every game was a road game—never a home court advantage, never a comfortable surrounding, rarely anything a new man would recognize or remember. I could see how it might be an exhausting way to live over the long haul, but I didn't care.

With a month left to play in the season, I was shifted to the Southern Unit of the Trotters. No longer was I on the opposition. I wasn't on the big team, the Eastern Unit, yet, but it was a start. Now I could really show my stuff.

When the season was over, I was told that I would have to try out before the next season. "Go back to Wilmington and wait for a train ticket to Chicago," Abe told me. That sounded all right with me because I hadn't seen a Globetrotter tryout before. I thought tryouts would be among all the guys on the various Trotter teams and the three traveling teams to see who would be placed where.

On the way home, I visited the hometown of my last Trotter roommate, Alvin Clinkscales. A friend of his picked us up at LaGuardia in April of 1955 and drove us into Bridgeport, Connecticut. The trees were green, the flowers in bloom. I thought it was one of the prettiest places I had ever seen. I knew immediately that it was a place I wanted to settle someday.

And I knew I wanted to marry Willye. I had seen her several times during the last two months—either she would come to see me when I was close to home or I would travel to see her.

I wasn't much for style or ceremony. When I got home, I gave her fair warning. I told her how tough life would be if she happened to marry a barnstorming professional comedy basketball player.

She said she knew. "If all those servicemen's wives could do it, and their husbands were not just gone but also in combat, I think I can handle it."

"So, what do you say we get married?"

We rode a Greyhound Bus across the state line into South Carolina where you could get all your permits and licenses and blood tests in a couple of hours rather than a couple of days. We came back the next morning married.

Her mother met us at the door, all ready to ask where we had been, but suspecting, too.

Before she had a chance to say anything, Willye told her matter-of-factly, "We got married, Mama."

"I know." She knew we had no money and nowhere to live, so she let us stay with her until I left for the tryouts in Chicago.

Even though we wanted our own place, Willye and I were truly happy and in love. Many an hour we spent hand in hand or arm in arm, strolling, enjoying the lazy Carolina evenings. We wanted a big family, a big house, a comfortable place to live.

We both, naturally, wanted more for ourselves and our kids than we had growing up. Had I known then the kind of money that would eventually be available to me, I might have been able to really plan and secure my future the way many highly paid athletes do. For then, it was enough to dream of being independent or being able to have what you need and want when you need or want it.

A few days before I was to leave for Chicago and the preseason Globetrotter tryouts, my old friend Son Gillyard told me he had re-enlisted for two terms and had been paid a twelve-hundred-dollar bonus. "I'm buyin' a Buick. Got to be in Michigan the day after you got to be in Chicago. How 'bout goin' with me? You'll save the fare. We can split the gas."

That sounded good. No one likes to travel alone. I was down to my last seventy dollars, and this way I could make it stretch farther.

Little did I know how quickly that seventy dollars would go in the next days or what a surprise awaited me in Chicago. All of the younger newer guys on the Globetrotter teams who played infrequently, like myself, had to face the fresh talent at the tryouts. My place in the organization wasn't at all secure, and I didn't even know it.

17

Getting There Was Half the Fun

The morning Son was to pick me up, I was awake early, packed and ready. I sat on Willye's mama's front porch waiting. And waiting. Finally, I lugged my suitcase to his house. He sat on the front steps, his head down.

"Hey, Son, you were gonna pick me up, man!"

"Oh, yeah, I was, wasn't I? Sorry. I got loaded last night. I don't feel so good."

"We got to get goin'. Where's the new car?"

He pointed to the side yard where sat the sorriest excuse for a Buick I'd ever seen. Rusted, tires bald, upholstery tattered, smelly, and mildewed. "Can you drive the first leg, Meadow? I'm shot."

I didn't say anything. I just tossed my suitcase in the back and slid behind the wheel. Son put his suitcase in the front seat next to me and crawled in the back, sliding my suitcase over the seat, too. He was asleep before I pulled out of the yard. His grandmother waved and waved from the door. I waved back.

"Hey, Son, the tank is almost empty."

"Can you catch this one, Meadow? I'll get the next one."

Two hundred miles later, it was time to gas up again. Son was out like a light. I smacked him on the thigh. "Your turn for gas and drivin', man."

He stirred. "Oh, Meadow, you got to give me a break. I feel awful. Drive one more leg, huh?"

"Awright, but you pay for the gas." He was asleep again. "Son, give me some money!"

He mumbled, "I'll make it up to you."

I was disgusted, watching my money dwindle, but I trusted Son. It was clear he was still suffering from his celebration the night before. But when I had to pay for more gas and drive the third leg, I'd had enough. I woke him and told him I had to get some sleep and that it was time for him to get involved.

He rubbed his eyes and sat up, running his hands through his hair. "Meadow, I got to tell ya, we got two problems. I spent all my money on this car and the party last night. And I don't know how to drive."

"How are you gonna get to Michigan?"

"I was hoping you'd teach me on the way."

"I'll teach you all right."

I was going to be down to next to nothing by the time I got to Chicago, where I was to spend the weekend alone in the Evans Hotel before training camp opened. I needed something to eat on. Son begged my forgiveness, and though I wasn't inclined to give it, what choice did I have?

I would have been all right, money-wise, if it hadn't been for the car battery. It died. Replacing it brought my funds down to under twenty dollars. The best I could figure, I was going to reach Chicago with five dollars and some change.

The next afternoon, after gassing up, checking the new battery, and adding some oil, I was doing about sixty-five on the turnpike when I noticed the hood vibrating. I wondered if it had closed properly. In another second, I knew. It flew up, obstructing my view. I pulled my foot off the accelerator and slid down the seat to see the road through the sliver of light. Suddenly, the hood was gone. I sat up and slammed on the brakes. In the rearview mirror I saw the hood floating down the highway. Luckily, there were no other cars close by.

I jogged back to get it, and we set it up so it was locked at the front, but not at the back. At least that way, it wouldn't catch the wind and fly away again. But the rattle was enough to drive you nuts!

By the time we got to Chicago, Son had learned to drive passably enough to get him to Michigan. I was, as I had predicted, down to five-plus dollars. Son pleaded for some of it. I gave him three. As he walked back to the car, a little black boy came by eating a hot dog. Son stepped next to him, surprised him with a quick, light slap to the face, and caught the hot dog as the boy dropped it. He jumped in the car and took off.

For years after that, every time I saw Son, I reminded him that he owed me fifty-three dollars. The more successful I became, the less he thought I needed it. He always told me he had invested it for me.

I bought as much food as I could afford, stocking up on potato chips and pop and a package of bologna. I had learned to eat like that as a kid to supplement my regular meals, and that would come in handy on the road for many years, too. We Trotters called that kind of fare Dutch for some reason, and it became a staple.

The Evans Hotel at Evans and Sixty-First Street was home headquarters for the Globetrotters. The players each had a room but shared a bathroom with the guy next door. It was kind of a quaint, black-run hotel, seven stories, a doorman, gift shop and liquor store, double beds, no TV or radio, just dresser, phone, and desk. To me, it was nice.

I sauntered into the tryouts that Monday as if I was returning to work. In the gym at a small Catholic high school on Sixty-First Street I saw 125 recent high-school and college graduates working to impress the Globetrotter management. They didn't look good. They looked great! I panicked.

I saw all those young guys flying, and I mean flying, through the air, slam dunking, rebounding, dribbling, shooting long jump shots, doing everything spectacular. It looked like a waterfall of balls going through the baskets. When we got down to real basketball, the flashiest looking ones knew the least about fundamentals. Still, I doubted I would even make one of the opposition teams. I didn't let it get me down. I decided to go down fighting, giving it all I had, as usual.

The best players in that camp were probably better than the NBA professionals. There were only a few blacks in the NBA then, and as now, for some reason blacks were better overall basketball players than whites.

By the end of two weeks, when the veterans came in for training camp, almost every rookie hopeful had been cut. It was hard to see some of them go, and there were others I was surprised hadn't made it. Every night we dragged ourselves back to the hotel after two separate four-hour sessions, eager to fall into bed and pray that we wouldn't be cut the next day.

I wasn't cut, and when the veterans arrived, I was ready to compete. It was one thing to survive. It was another to win a spot on the big team, the Eastern Unit, which was everyone's goal. If you didn't make the Eastern Unit, you wanted to make either the Western or the Southern Unit. Short of that, you played for the opposition and tried to work your way up.

During that training camp, I learned the history of the Globetrotters. Abe wanted the promising young players, the ones he hoped would be with him for years, to know what the Trotters were all about. Abe formed the team in 1926. As a twenty-six-year-old entrepreneur, he managed the Savoy Big Five, a black basketball team recruited to play in Chicago's new Savoy Ballroom.

When rollerskating overtook basketball in the Savoy, Abe renamed the team Harlem (to make it clear they were black) Globetrotters (because he planned to tour Illinois and wanted to look big-time). That first year, 1927, they traveled by car, slept only where they were allowed, and played local teams for a guarantee of twenty-five dollars and 50 percent of the gate.

At the end of the season they divided up the money and returned to their normal jobs. Their record was 101–6. Once, the following year, when they won a game 112–5, Saperstein instituted comedy and ballhandling tricks to keep the fans from being bored. Abe himself sometimes took to the court, and the team would cakewalk around him while he made a set shot. He had one law: The Trotters never clowned at the expense of winning.

In 1940 the Trotters won the national pro title from the Chicago Bruins in Chicago Stadium before twenty-one thousand fans. With a new bus and sparkling new uniforms, they became a big-city phenomenon and started to make some money. They got so big they had to divide into two and then three units.

In 1950 they played in Madison Square Garden in New York and became a yearly attraction. By the time I joined them in 1955, they had been around almost thirty years and were the best, as well as the best-known, basketball organization in the world.

This, then, was the team I had dreamed of for years. But by now I had quickly gone from thinking I was an automatic starter on the big club, the Eastern Unit, to realizing that I was in grave danger of trudging back to Wilmington with a few memories.

Training camp required almost all of my energy, but I worked out in my hotel room, standing before the mirror, practicing my moves. I even practiced a few comical facial expressions and funny ways of walking and holding the ball. I would have been embarrassed for anyone to know that I had my sights set even higher than making the Eastern Unit, even higher than starting on the big club. I wanted to be the lead clown someday. As long as my dream was a long shot to start with, and as long as I wouldn't be deterred, I figured I might as well go for it all.

During training camp, I did everything but play lead clown with the big club. I worked out with the Stars, with the West, the South, and the East. I subbed, I played one of the running positions, I dribbled, whatever they wanted. Some of the veterans tried to tell me that the only reason I had played in Europe was because Abe could pay me part-time rates and didn't have to fly me over there.

It may have been true. The longer I'm in the sports and entertainment business and see how much it costs to put a team on the road, the more believable their story becomes. But I kept telling myself that not just any black basketball player in Europe was chosen. I was, and for a reason.

When I found myself moping around the hotel or having trouble falling asleep, I lectured myself just like my dad or my coaches would have. *You giving up, Meadow? Is this it? The end of the line? If you were going to leave, you should have left when you saw all those rookies trying out! You survived that, didn't you? Aren't you the kid who said nothing would get in the way of his goal? The kid who practiced alone if he had to, to turn himself from a skinny little guy into a real ballplayer?*

I'd almost psyche myself up to steal a starting job with the Eastern Unit when the training camp sessions would start and I'd see how impossible my dream was. I wanted to make it. I was determined to make it. And the regulars, the veterans, seemed just as determined to see me *not* make it.

They weren't outwardly hostile. They weren't mean. They just played rough and made me earn every rebound, every steal, every dribble and pass and shot. Worse, they ignored me. They knew who I was. They knew Abe had allowed the unusual, had put me in a real game for my tryout, liked what he saw, and wanted me to make it. But they pretended they didn't know. They treated me like any other nobody lucky enough to survive rookie tryout and wind up at training camp. In their minds, I didn't belong there, and I was getting plenty of signals. It only made me more determined.

If a player could unseat another by sheer force of will, I would. I wish I could say I was confident that my name would still be on the "keep" list posted outside the gym every day. I tried to look nonchalant when I glanced at it. In truth, I breathed a sigh of relief every time I saw it. I hurt for my friends and acquaintances whose names disappeared overnight.

When that happened, there were no questions asked and few good-byes. It was humiliating, disappointing, and embarrassing. Some guys would tell you, then pack and leave. But most just turned in their gear, picked up their travel money to get them home, and slipped away. If it happened to me, I was sure it would be a mistake. It would be because someone wasn't watching, wasn't noticing that I was giving it all I had.

Finally, it was announced that the names on the sheet the next day would be the ones who had made the organization, and their assignments would be listed as well. My first wish, of course, was to be somewhere on that sheet. I was. Second, I wanted to be assigned to the big club. I wasn't. Third, I wanted to start. I didn't. I was listed as a sub. But I made it.

I was assigned to the Southern Unit where Sam Wheeler was the lead showman. Sam played center, which meant he controlled the ball, dished it off, maintained constant chatter, and kept everyone laughing. He was the star of most of the reems (gags). I was playing mostly in the third quarter, learning my trade, but I could see that the top clown was the guy who had the most fun.

The Trotter teams didn't have guards as such, but three men

who brought the ball up the court in a weaving pattern. As the pivot man (or center) set up near the free-throw line and the other big man moved to one of the corners, the three running men brought the ball up, bounce passing, passing behind their backs, weaving, hardly dribbling. The three fastest and surest ball-handlers were assigned this job, and it was always impressive.

It was amazing to see how quickly we got upcourt that way. Then the ball went in to the pivot man, who kept dishing it back out to the bobbing and weaving threesome. Eventually, of course, when you least expected it, the big man in the corner or one of the three running men made a dash for the hoop. The pivot man hit him with a deadeye pass for the basket.

The opposition was to allow us to do our skits and gags and also to allow for a free pass into the pivot man. Otherwise, they were to play as hard as they could and try to beat us. They tried everything to get rebounds, intercept passes, and beat us by playing tough defense. It's a myth either that we are upset or that they are in trouble if they beat us. Abe Saperstein never wanted us to lose, and we tried not to, but every once in a great while, it happened. Some of our opposition teams were made up of pretty good players, after all. Our records against less than the world's best is not important. Good basketball, entertainment, and laughter were what we were after.

It was so much fun just to be involved that I drank in every experience. I wanted to learn everything so that when my chance came, I would be ready to do whatever was asked of me on the big club. Every unit did basically the same routines, gags, or reems. We started, of course, with the magic circle where a half-dozen or so of the best ballhandlers led the way out onto the floor and passed the ball around, faking tosses, bounce passing, rolling the ball down our arms, holding it behind our backs with our elbows, drop-kicking it, whatever came to mind. We did all this to the strains of "Sweet Georgia Brown."

My first time in the magic circle was frightening. I felt like I'd forgotten everything I'd ever learned about trick ballhandling. I worried I would forget what to do with the ball when it came to me, hoped against hope that a pass wouldn't surprise me and bounce off my chest.

I knew when the guys were faking and when they were really passing, but I found myself flinching. Suddenly, the ball came to me, and everything came back. I knew exactly what to do. The music and the crowd noise helped. I let the ball roll down my arm, across my neck and to my other hand, then started it back the other way. When it got to my neck, I let it fall behind me, and I kicked it to a teammate while the crowd screamed and the music got louder and louder. Finally I *was* a Globetrotter.

18

The Lead Clown

The first of Willye's and my five children, Meadow George Lemon IV, was born in 1956 when I was in Yugoslavia. Each summer, the ten best or most promising Globetrotters from all thirty players in the three units were selected to tour Europe. That summer I was asked to go, and I couldn't refuse even though our baby was due. I was on the road to the top.

Willye wasn't happy that I hadn't been able to be there for George's birth. Neither was I, of course, but it was something we had discussed and was one of the prices of the kind of life I had chosen. I thought Willye had been resigned to that, and this should have been a clue to the trouble ahead for us. Willye was still living with her mother. When I finally got home to see baby George, I knew it was time for us to move to our own place.

We took a train to New York and then to Bridgeport, but I was so tired from the road, she was so tired from having recently had a baby, and George was so tired because he *was* a baby, we were asleep when the conductor announced Bridgeport.

By the time we woke up, the train was ready to pull out. In a daze, we gathered up everything and hurried from the car, just as the train started rolling again. We went to Alvin Clinkscales's home. He was going to help us find a hotel room until we could rent an apartment, but his mother, May Sally, wouldn't hear of it. "You stayin' right here till you find a place."

Eventually, we located an apartment, but on my low salary, we couldn't afford much furniture. Several creditors checked with

Abe, who said he had long-range plans for me, so I was able to get a loan to buy a car.

While I was on the road again the next season, the landlord told Willye that if we had enough money to buy a car, we had enough for a raise in the rent. Willye hit the roof. She rightfully thought that was unfair. She knew we had gone into debt for the car and our few pieces of furniture, so she refused to pay more for the apartment.

She hardly knew how to drive, didn't have a license, but she put the furniture in storage, packed up little George, and drove back to Wilmington. Several months later, when I got off the road again, we went back to Connecticut to try again. Through a succession of apartments and rooming houses, we kept searching for a house. Willye was pressuring me to find one before I returned to the road, and I wanted one, too.

The problem was we didn't have much money in 1957. We couldn't have bought a doll house for what I had in the bank. One of the Trotter promoters, Al Warner, had told me, "It's not important how much you have, but how much people think you have." I put on my best suit and went looking for loans. Abe helped, and we put together enough for a down payment on a decent little abandoned house in Fairfield, an expensive suburb of Westport. A lawyer had gone through a divorce and wound up with two homes. This one was nice, but neglected, and had waist-high weeds in the yard. I liked the potential. Willye didn't. I knew I had no choice. I started the process.

Alvin and some of his relatives and friends got to work with me on that house. Willye didn't want anything to do with it. She couldn't see the potential. I couldn't believe it; we were two nobodies from nowhere with a chance to move uptown, but she wasn't satisfied. Every few days, Willye would come by and warily look it over. When the yard was finally down to two inches of healthy grass and the inside was getting spruced up, she started saying, "Look how nice my house is startin' to look."

That made me feel better, but tearing myself away from my wife and baby was more difficult than ever that fall.

I was again the eager student of Sam Wheeler, who was a friendly and patient teacher. I watched closely. I wanted to be funny. I wanted to be the lead showman. I wanted to make the big club. And I wanted the clown spot on that team. I don't know what inspired Abe to move me to the big club midway through the season, and I didn't stop to think about it. I had worked hard, that's all I knew. When I was pulled aside, I thought I was in trouble. "Lemon, Abe wants you in Chicago."

I was petrified. "What'd I do?"

"Beats me. But congratulations. You'll be traveling with the big club."

"The Eastern Unit? Are you serious?"

"We don't joke about things like that, kid."

"I'm up there for good?"

"Well, I imagine that's up to Abe—and you. Better get goin'."

When I joined the Eastern Unit, I realized I'd just been called up to solve a temporary situation. But what an opportunity! Bob (Showboat) Hall was the lead man on the big club at that time, and he was sick. Abe wanted me to substitute for Bob as lead clown.

I couldn't believe it. Everyone on the team wanted the job, and I was not only one of the youngest and least experienced players but from the Southern Unit.

I was so nervous, I nearly got sick. But when the game started, when it was time for some reems and I felt my teammates looking to me to start things off, I was into it. Man, I mean I was there.

From somewhere deep inside me came a joy and even a voice that I can only use while I'm on the court in the heat of a game. I made the most of it. I was ready. I played the pivot, dishing the ball off, starring in most of the reems, and in one sense emceeing the whole game with my incessant falsetto chatter.

When the coach, my teammates, and the fans took notice that I was the man in the middle, on the spot, with the ball, making things happen, I got high with the experience. I wanted to make people laugh so hard they'd burst. I was making people happy. *Me*. Meadow George Lemon III from Wilmington, North Carolina! The nervousness was gone. I felt that capacity crowd having fun because of me, but no one was having a better time than I was.

In those early years, we played local teams made up of construction workers or miners, even football players, and what they lacked in basketball finesse, they made up for in strength and desire to win. I had to develop my hook shot into a long, high shot that I took on the run, usually away from the basket. I simply got tired of having my bell rung every night, and I had had it with being bumped on every shot.

In the last five seconds of that game I made a half-court hook shot on my first try. By the time the opposition team took the ball out, the game was over. I knew I had played well.

I spent a week traveling with the Eastern Unit, and then, once Showboat was feeling better, Abe sent me back to the Southern Unit. My career as clown had been short-lived, but I'd loved every minute of it.

After the 1957–58 season was over, Abe Saperstein called me at home and asked me to come to New York for a benefit. I didn't know till I got there that he was giving me my final test for lead clown by putting me before the biggest crowd that would ever see me play.

I don't remember what the function was, but the benefit drew a capacity crowd of sixty-five thousand in Yankee Stadium, and dozens of acts entertained the crowd—circus acts, comedians, music groups, you name it.

We set the court up on the baseball diamond. I was glad that I'd practiced that smile of mine in front of the mirror for the past few years. I had known someday my smile would have to be seen from the stands in a basketball arena. Now I faced an audience that seemed to be sitting miles away in the Yankee Stadium bleachers.

My smile always gets to an audience, and it did that day. Once the spectators start laughing, my smile gets broader and broader. Although they don't know it, I smile because the audience is actually throwing a smile at me. I'm really throwing it back to them. That day the crowd and I laughed from the first five minutes on. I just let that great big smile take over.

Near the end we went into our baseball routine. I was the batter, my fists the bat, a basketball the baseball.

A member of the team threw the ball at me—or behind me, I should say.

"Strike one!" the umpire shouted.

"But, but did you *see* that?" I yelled back. "He threw the ball behind me."

"Shut up and bat up," came the answer.

The "pitcher" wound up and threw a ball that hit my shoulder and bounced off.

"S-T-R-I-K-E TWO!" the umpire screamed.

"Strike two?" I turned and walked back to the umpire. "He struck me. Didn't you see that?"

"Get back up there," he growled.

"All right, all right. But watch me knock this one out of here."

The pitcher spit on his hands and on the ball. He wound up.

"Hey," I yelled at the umpire, "he's getting ready to throw me a spit ball."

"Hit it on the dry side then!"

"You don't understand," I insisted. "When that guy spits on a ball, there isn't a dry side!"

I wound up for the pitch, which was soft so I could blast it. BAMMM! The ball sailed beyond the court. Guys scrambled onto the grass to get it.

By the time a fielder retrieved the ball and sent it to the catcher, I was turning third base in my famous high-stepping strut. Now it was between the two of us.

I started chattering at him. Suddenly, I pointed in the other direction and shouted, "Hey, there's Superman!"

The catcher turned around, and I slid between his legs for a home run! I always like to say that I hit an inside-the-park home run in Yankee Stadium.

We ended the game with my usual half-court hook shot. I had pulled out every trick I knew at that time, and it worked. I was the lead clown for more than two decades after that.

19

On the Road Again and Again

Everybody knows how tough it is to live on the road, but I have to say that as a young ballplayer, I loved it. It was everything I hoped it would be. We had fun, we had pride, we cared about each other.

The bus—not the big Greyhound-type cruisers we enjoy today, but the school-bus style—and hotels became our homes. People who saw the Globetrotter movies, *Go, Man, Go!* and *The Harlem Globetrotters*, got the impression that we traveled, ate, and slept on the bus. Sometimes we did, but whenever we could find a hotel that would take us in, we crashed for a while.

Some of those hotels were nice. Most were not. Occasionally, when Abe had carefully booked us within a several-hundred-mile radius of a hotel, we would make that our headquarters for a while. One of the earliest of my years on the road was spent at the old Foster Hotel in Indianapolis. This hotel was bad.

The beds were two-inch pallets on sprung springs. You got a very thin blanket, two sheets, and—if you were lucky—a pillow. There was such a draft coming through the half-inch gaps between window and window sill, and the radiators produced more noise than heat, that you had to go to bed fully clothed, coat included.

One late fall night, a bone-chilling rain came through the ceiling, and I had to round up a bunch of trash cans to use as drop buckets so my room wouldn't flood. Andy Johnson was my roommate at the time, and he somehow thought keeping the room from flooding was my responsibility.

At first, Andy treated me like the rookie I was. He was a man of over six five and about 245 pounds who was one of the strongest basketball players in the game. We called him Handy Andy because he played all positions. He intimidated a lot of people, and I guess he was among those who thought I wasn't ready to be on the big club, as young as I was. I got the silent treatment a lot, and whatever he said, went. We pooled our money to buy Dutch—meat and cheese and fruit and cookies and stuff like that—then he ate more than half of it.

He was a nightclubber, which wasn't my scene early on. I was so conscientious, not to mention scared that everyone might be right about my limited talent, that I stayed in the room and practiced my moves and facial expressions in the mirror. I don't know how many hotel room windows I broke all over the country before I perfected my skills with a basketball.

Andy would come back after midnight from nightclubbing and slam the door, turn the lights on, slam drawers, and generally act like I wasn't sleeping in there. One night, I'd had enough. As soon as he came in and turned on the light, I leaped from the bed, went behind him, and locked the door.

He looked amused. "What you up to, rookie?"

"Okay, big fella, it's gonna be you and me. We're gonna get this thing straight. You come in here every night, wakin' me up, treatin' me like dirt. . . ." I dove at him and wrestled him to the floor between the beds. I was furious, pumped up, ready to kill. What was maddening was that he was giggling. He couldn't believe it! I was tickling him in more ways than one. In one easy move, he rolled over, and I wound up underneath him, my shoulders pinned to the floor. He had me by at least sixty-five pounds. I squirmed and threatened, but I wasn't going anywhere. He was laughing. "You crazy, Meadow. Crazy!"

He could have chewed me up and spit me out, or at least beat the daylights out of me. I feared that at any moment he would realize that I had ambushed him and make me regret it. All he would have had to do was to haul off and clobber me on the head. "You promise to get up like a good boy and go back to bed, and I'll let you up."

I relaxed, and he let me up. I went back to bed without a word, but he also turned off the light and got undressed in the dark, quieter than ever. It was that way from then on. The next morning we were buddies. He learned that I had rights and was foolish enough to stick up for them. I learned he had compassion for a pencil-thin rookie he could have broken in two. We were good friends from then on. Andy eventually made the NBA.

One of the first times I went nightclubbing with the guys was after we had played a night game in a community just outside of Indianapolis. We got in earlier than usual, but the heat was off in the hotel and the cold breezes blew in every room. That night it seemed everyone just changed, turned around, and headed out to the club.

The club was on the second floor of an old, run-down two-story building, and to get to it you had to walk up a long flight of wood stairs. The group I was with got there a little late, and when we started up the stairs, we saw Lee Garner, the tallest player on the team, at the top, arguing with a midget. To get the full impact of how hilarious this was, you have to realize that Lee Garner was six eleven. He had to duck going through standard doorways.

I don't know what started it, but that pint-sized man was giving him a hard time. I cringed when big Lee drew back on the midget. I knew he was gonna knock him to tomorrow. He caught that little guy in the chest and drove him up the top three stairs to the landing. I thought he had killed him. So did Lee.

He looked down to smirk at us, but the grin quickly stiffened into a frown. From behind him, the midget screamed, "Big boy, you're in trouble now."

A giant couldn't have said those words with more power and determination. Lee turned to stare as the midget took a run at him. Lee swore, twirled back around and bounded down the stairs four at a time. The rest of us pressed ourselves against the walls on either side of the stairs and made room for the big guy.

Lee blasted through the front door, and here came the midget, muttering, "I'll . . . that black giant when I catch him." We almost collapsed from laughter and followed him out the door. By the time he got outside, Lee was galloping about two blocks away. The tiny man screamed threats at him and cruised along with his choppy steps. Lee kept running, and we laughed till we cried.

When we got back to the hotel after midnight, Lee was reading the paper in the lobby. "That dwarf ain't with ya, is he?"

We assured him he wasn't. "You afraida that midget, Garner?"

He nodded slowly. "I give a man everything I've got and he comes at me again, I get outta there."

I was still chuckling the next morning. What a sight! For the rest of the season, every time one of us would think of Lee or the midget or the incident, we'd tell it all over again.

The sorriest hotel we ever stayed in was a black-owned place in Jacksonville, Florida. The managers treated us like dirt. The woman kept assuming that we would be as bad as the group of roadies that Sam Cooke had brought with him a few months before. The problem was, we had a lot of games within a 250-mile radius, so Abe had us booked in there for quite a while.

After six o'clock in the evening, the phones in the rooms were turned off. One night we asked the woman if she would call cabs for us to get to the local high school for our game. Getting our group to the game was no simple matter.

Besides the ten Globetrotters, the eight opposition players, and assorted road personnel, there was also our half-time entertainment—the well-known singer-entertainer Cab Calloway and Pegleg Bates, the one-legged dancer who was one of the greatest tap dancers I've ever seen, despite his peg leg. That man could jump over my head when he leaped across the floor!

The woman looked at all of us standing in a corner of what she called her lobby and promptly called one cab!

"Lady, we got to have at least a half-dozen taxis!"

"I'm not spendin' all my time callin' cabs for you! Call 'em yourself!"

"The phones are off!"

"Use the one in the lobby." We crowded around it. Three companies said they would send two each. None came. We wound up hitchhiking to the game.

The next night we were bused 250 miles to our most remote game during that stay. Cab Calloway had managed to get a car to drive to and from the game so he started back to the hotel before the team. When we returned at 2:00 A.M., Cab and his pianist stood outside the couple's bedroom.

Cab was screaming, "We've been here an hour, and now the team has arrived! You have to let us in!"

She screamed right back. "If you can't be here at a godly hour, you don't sleep here! That's all!"

When the whole team gathered around the window and pleaded with her to "let us in tonight and kick us out tomorrow," she sent her husband out to unlock the front door.

A hotel in Tampa was the only one I ever stayed in that had bedbugs that would attack you. You know how they're supposed to run from the light and run from people? Not these buggers. I felt 'em crawlin' on me in the night, so I jumped up and turned on the light to get rid of 'em. They came at me! I stepped up on a chair with a rolled-up newspaper and beat 'em off as they climbed up the legs. I swear.

On the other hand, we occasionally stayed at some great hotels in the big cities where black entertainers playing in the area would stay. It was a thrill to rub shoulders with the big names and to have hotels that treated you like stars. It was also gratifying to see signs welcoming back "The Harlem Globetrotters." Those were the days.

Among my fondest memories are the times when Duke Cumberland and Ducky Moore entertained the crowd. These two old gents were pros. Duke had played with the Trotters when he was younger and years later in a pinch.

They drove the bus, managed the business, and took care of details. But when a stadium filled up early or the crowd was restless before we were scheduled to take the court, these guys might come walking out in their suits and ties and start shooting. The crowd didn't know what to think. Were these men Globetrotters? Of course, they were middle-aged and out of shape. Duke had a big belly and had been bald since he was young.

As the crowd quieted, Duke and Ducky talked to each other so everyone could hear. They shot from half-court sometimes making ten or more in a row. "Ducky, baby! If it hits anything but the bottom of the net, I don't even want it. You can have it."

They banked shots off the walls, off the ceiling, talking to the fans, talking to each other. They competed to see who could make the most of twenty or the most in a row. Their shots were amazing, and the repartee had the people howling. There were nights when we didn't know if we could follow them, they were that good.

Those guys were also teachers, instructing us in the finer points of the game and in media and public relations. I learned a lot from them and loved to hear them talk of the old days, the Negro baseball leagues and, especially, how to pick up women. They found girls on the streets, in the shops, in the restaurants, in hotel lobbies, in the stands, you name it.

Their approach was novel, and it wouldn't surprise me if it was still in use today. The sting was a thing they called Globetrotter Queen. An unsuspecting young girl with stars in her eyes heard that she could compete with many others for the chance to be Globetrotter Queen and win a trip to Europe, five thousand dollars in cash, and a ten-thousand-dollar mink coat.

Duke and Ducky traded off being cameraman, once they got a girl into their hotel room for the official entry photo. They had a big Brownie camera with a bulb that popped when it flashed, film or no film. "Okay, dear, now you have to give us a little cheesecake. That's it." *Flash! Pop!*

If the girl refused to cooperate in the photo session, the two commiserated loudly about how they would "just have to forget about this one." Duke was a guy who could cry at the drop of a hat. Whenever he didn't get his own way, he hung his head and cried big tears. That often worked with the girls, but he didn't get far with the team. We were onto his trick.

During one of those early road trips, a good ballplayer named Josh Crider started adding Lark to my name. He said it in a slow staccato. "Meadow-lark!" The other guys started picking up on it. Abe was amused by it, and the next thing I knew, his promotional material was hawking his lead comic as Meadowlark Lemon.

20

Abe

To me, no combination could compare with the teams we had in the late fifties and early sixties. The friendships, the laughs, the stories couldn't be topped. But we used to go to the floor every night hungry and mad because of the tough lives we lived. If a guy scored against you, and you suspected he had had a decent meal before the game, watch out! We had to love basketball to go through what we went through.

I mean, we played under all kinds of conditions, all over the world. In Germany we played at the bottom of a drained swimming pool with people watching from above. The echo was unbelievable, not to mention the strange bounce on the gently sloping floor.

In Italy we played on plywood sheets that covered an ice-skating rink. It sleeted, and the boards separated. We kept warm by alternating five guys on the "floor" with five in the locker room every few minutes.

Once we played on a court made of table tops! We played on soccer fields where we chalked off the basketball court so we wouldn't have to run the length of the field. Our road managers—and we players—had to be ready on short notice to construct poles and backboards so the rims and nets could go up. We never knew what the surface would be.

In the south of France we played in a bull ring (the longest distance between baskets ever—approximately fifty yards!) where we had to dribble through blood and other unmentionables. We played on grass—it wasn't short—and even on the deck of a battleship. I remember playing on a clay tennis court when it rained and left us ankle deep in the red stuff.

We put down a portable floor and fences so we could play on beaches in Italy. We had to find rocks and bags of dirt to secure the poles. After games like that, we didn't even shower and change until we had helped tear down the portable stadium. All was not sweetness and light.

But the toughest part about traveling with the Trotters was trying to understand Abe Saperstein. Five-foot-three-and-a-half and who knows how many pounds, he was about as different as he could be from his ballplayers. Most of us were tall, thin, and black. He was Jewish, and he smarted when people called him a slave owner or a racist. He hired blacks when it was unfashionable, and he liked to think of us as his children. He used to say, "There are two things you can get fired for: not stopping to look at the basket and messing with my women."

He was a strange guy, and I developed a love-hate relationship with him. On the one hand, he was the guy who made my dream come true. On the other, I felt I had to treat him as a father figure, a Santa Claus, to get anything out of him. I was in no position to demand or even ask. I had to be subservient and beg and plead to get a break.

Abe liked to tell people he was a great coach. Occasionally, he almost convinced us. Once we were down by 20 points in the fourth quarter, and he told us he would win the game through coaching strategy. He put in a new man in a makeshift uniform, and the guy couldn't miss. We won, and Abe took the credit.

At other times he would get out on the practice floor and demonstrate the nuances of the game, like he knew them and we didn't. He would show us how to protect the ball in the pivot, standing there all stubby and short with one of our six eight or six eleven guys standing behind him. "Now try to take the ball from me!"

Any of us could have had it in a second, but there was no job security in that. Whoever the stooge was would make some vigorous but halfhearted attempt to touch the ball and give up. "I can't, Skipper. I can't do it."

Abe would grin and toss the ball to someone. "See?" We would all nod.

When the crowds were huge, Abe wasn't happy. I always assumed it was because he was afraid we would figure out how much money he was making on us and we would try to hit him up for some of it. The bigger the crowd, in his mind, the worse we played. We couldn't do anything right. If we won big, we spoiled everything because the game was boring. If our reems brought the house down, he'd tell us our basketball had taken a back seat to comedy.

Once in Paris, we led a team 56–0 with a second to go before the half. He loved that. It was a blowout, but it was unique. Something special. Then their guard threw the ball with one hand from one end of the court to the basket at the opposite end. Miraculously, the ball went in! Abe was furious. We had let down and embarrassed him. He liked to call us Oscars, for some reason. I guess he was accusing us of acting.

The best game I ever played as a Globie wasn't good enough for Abe. I had to have scored nearly 50 points, played tough D, and all my gags were screamers. People were on the floor, laughing so hard. We won an interesting if not close game, and I glowed in the aftermath. I was called to Abe's hotel room. I just knew he was going to praise me, maybe give me a raise, maybe slip me a few dollars for some fun. Instead he ranted and raved about my game, my laziness, my slowness. He warned me that I had better pull my game together.

That was all I needed to hear. I was enraged to the point of tears, but I could not, would not, let him see me break down. If he or I had said one more word in that room, I'd have popped him and cried both.

I stormed out, determined to quit the team and go home. Things were really bad between Willye and me by then, and I was starting to agree with her that this life on the road had caused it. I certainly didn't intend to stay where I wasn't wanted. I called the airport. A flight to New York was scheduled for nine the next morning. I reserved a seat.

I was packed and ready to go the next morning when I ran into Abe and a few of his friends. I decided not to say anything, to just nod and head for a taxi. I mourned the end of a relationship.

Abe caught my arm and introduced me to his friends. "And this, this is the best Globetrotter I've ever had. A super player, the consummate showman, a loyal team member, and a good friend. Meadowlark Lemon. We couldn't survive without him." He slipped me a hundred-dollar bill and whispered, "Have yourself some fun tonight after the game, big guy."

You figure it. I smiled, thanked him, went back to my room, unpacked, and had another great game that night—and some fun afterward.

No doubt Abe was a genius and a motivator. He handled all the promotion, made loans, kept players from forming cliques by switching roommates whenever he felt it necessary, and basically held our futures in his hands. That was power he used for and against people, and he left a lot of people with security—to his credit. When he died, he left me with a job. Not much money at that time, but a job and a future anyway. Several of his long-time players were given other jobs in the organization when their playing days ended. He could be that kind of a guy. There were times when I was convinced that he was trying to break me. He pitted me against great showmen and continually made me earn my spot.

Abe was good with the media. He stayed in touch with all his old friends in the press and the entertainment world, people like Bob Hope and Ed Sullivan. He was a real promoter and P.R. man, the best, despite whatever character faults I or any other Trotter ever thought he had.

There were times when he might sidle up to a player after a good game and slip three or four hundred dollars into his pocket. Once during the early sixties, on the bus to New London, Connecticut, after a game in Madison Square Garden, Abe produced two shopping bags full of cash and passed out bonuses to the players. I got about five hundred dollars.

So, there were times when his compassion came through.

He taught me a lot of things. At the time, I didn't realize all that I learned from him or all the pressure he was under. He did what he had to do to put on the best possible show. I thought the team was it, the end-all, the show itself. I didn't realize until I tried to put the Bucketeers, my own comedy basketball team, on the road how expensive it was and how many behind-the-scenes people it required. If they don't handle the business for you, you got no show.

Abe dreamed up a tour for us that put us up against the recently graduated college and university stars. He called it the All-America Tour, and it was a big draw. People loved to see the college stars play us, but at first it wasn't really much of a match up. The kids were good, but we were a team. We knew how to win, even when we were having fun. We beat them by 25 and put on a full show.

The college stars complained that they were being shown up, and they threatened to go home. These guys were each making a hundred a game. We were making time and a half, and it didn't add up to that much. But Abe must have thought they were important to the show to pay them that much, and he wasn't about to have them leave in a huff.

He told us he would give every man twenty-five dollars if we could beat the college all-stars by just 1 point. It was ludicrous, but we were hungry for strokes, for attention, for money, for anything. It's not easy winning a game by 1 point. You need to maintain a 3-point lead and then let the other team get 2 in the closing seconds, without fouling them and letting them tie it. You can't let them get a 1-point lead and try to win it yourself with a last second 2-pointer, because if you miss, you're dead.

Well, we did it. Somehow, we made it work. It took so much energy that our reems weren't the best, but we did what we were told and pocketed the cash. The next night we played the college all-stars in Detroit. The kids were dead tired from playing every day, but we were long used to the roughest schedules. Abe reminded us to keep the game close again. I had to ask, "You mean, win by 1 again?"

He smiled. We did our best. In the end, something went haywire, and we lost. Abe was furious. At least he didn't make us pay him his money back.

The last time we played the Minneapolis Lakers, Abe wouldn't let Herman Taylor or me play because he didn't want to risk our getting hurt in what he considered an exhibition game. The truth was, of course, that all our games were exhibition games. What he wanted was an excuse if we lost. He could say he didn't have his top guys, his stars, in the game.

We would have won anyway, if it hadn't been for a freak injury. One of our best players pulled a muscle early in the game, forcing Andy Johnson to play the whole way. He was so tired that he missed 19 or 21 free throws, and even though he scored 38 points and we led by as many as 11 in the fourth quarter, we lost by 4.

I remember when the end was near for Abe. He fell asleep on the bench. I leaned over and put a hand on his shoulder. "You'd better go back to the hotel and get some sleep, Skip." He agreed, which was rare. And he left. The last time I saw him was in his hotel room in Los Angeles. He told me how tired he was.

On March 15, 1966, I heard the phone ring at the scorers' table and knew somehow it was bad news. In the locker room, a tearful Parnell Woods broke the news. "Skip has died. He would have wanted you to finish the game and the tour, and no one is expected to attend the funeral." That didn't seem right to me, but we abided by his wishes.

All of us had quit on Abe at one time or another, but he was a guy who was hard to hate for long. He could put the screws to you, then show you love in the next breath. None of us could figure him. None of us really liked him, but for some reason we loved him. I know he died doing what he loved most, running the Harlem Globetrotters.

21

The Clown Prince

Autographs. A lot of stars grow to hate signing them. I never have. I've always loved it. I admit that I have to wear a certain public face, a distant, sometimes vacant frown. It developed subconsciously over the years as I learned that the more open and approachable you appear, the more people will take advantage of you inappropriately.

I don't go around in public looking like I know I'm somebody and welcoming the masses to get close for a look or a touch. I go about my business. My look makes people need a little courage to work for the reaction they want from me, but that's all the qualifying they have to do. Anyone who recognizes me and speaks to me in a polite manner gets an autograph and whatever small talk I have time for.

I don't give kisses. I don't respond well to people who shove a piece of paper between my face and my fork. I don't leave my meal to go to someone else's table on a request that comes via the waitress. But I love people. Asking for autographs is their way of saying hi, and I want to say hi back.

Nine out of ten people are nice about it. They don't demand. They don't treat you like a piece of meat. The occasional person who thanks me for the laughs or the thrills over the years gets the best reaction. I know that it's the people who made me. They appreciated what I tried to do.

I'm amused when I get mistaken for Bill Cosby or Nipsy Russell. Like most well-known faces, I also get a lot of people who start with, "Wait a minute, I know you. You're somebody, aren't you? Don't tell me. Oh, okay, tell me."

"Bob Hope." They laugh. Then I tell them the truth. "Meadowlark Lemon."

"No, that's not it. . . ."

One time I had a little stomach ailment on the road, which required frequent trips to the facilities. I was jogging toward the washroom in an airport when I heard a man calling me. I really couldn't stop. I hurried into a stall, but he had seen me. He thrust a piece of paper under the wall. "Mr. Lemon, I'm sorry to bother you, but I'm late for my plane and my son would never forgive me if I didn't get your autograph." I had to laugh. He got his autograph.

I don't like it when people catch me coming out of the shower dripping wet, but I usually sign just to avoid trouble. A woman asked for an autograph while I was on the bench during a game, and when I turned her down, she bopped me with her purse. The crowd loved it until the cops carted her away.

Lots of people ask for autographs for someone else, usually a son or daughter. I once had a woman tell me, "It's not for me. It's for my French poodle!"

In Ogden, Utah, I left an arena by the wrong exit and was mobbed by fans. By the time I signed all the autographs, the bus had left without me. I had to ask if anyone could drive me thirty miles to the hotel. A few were happy to do it, and they got more than an autograph.

There have been better basketball players than Meadowlark Lemon over the years, maybe even better Harlem Globetrotters. But I can say without apology that no one ever loved the game, the gags, the crowd, the life more than I did.

I mean, I just flat loved it.

The favorite routines have been passed down from one team and one clown to the next over the years. We pretend to play football. We throw water on each other, then on the fans. Or will it be confetti?

Then on the fast break, I climb on the shoulders of our tallest player, take a pass, and score the easiest dunk shot ever as the buzzer sounds the end of the quarter.

During the game, we constantly remind ourselves that quality basketball comes first. Nothing is funny if the Trotters can't put the ball through the hoop and get a lead that allows us to have some fun. Late in each quarter we start with the reems. If there is no scoreboard clock, as in many places overseas, we signal each other with our own lingo. "Pair of deuces" means there are four minutes to go. "Let's sell something" means it's time to be funny. "Let's get outta here" means we have to finish our last reem before the end of the quarter.

Over the years I've developed a few lines to indicate some of my own routines. The "Connie C." is an overhead pass play. "Clean 'em up" is when I get fouled. "Raise 'em up" means I'm going to kick a pass. "Hey" means I'm going to shoot off my head—at least three baskets or so in a row.

I'm injured at least twice during most games. Each time I feel like I'm getting prepared for the Oscars. I fall, no matter how slight my contact with a member of the opposition is. When I was young, I used to fall from way up high. (I've accumulated a lot of bone spurs in my elbow that way, so now I tend to do a spin and roll onto the floor.)

When Wilt Chamberlain was playing with us in the early years, he usually carried me off the court. He'd pick me up like I was his little boy. Sometimes he even threw me up in the air like a rag doll. That guy's unbelievably strong!

Near the end of the game I get hurt again. This time a couple of the guys carry me off the court. Instead of letting the ball go, I hold onto it so I can substitute a trick ball for the regulation one for the next reem.

"Awwww! Ohhhh! OOOwwww!" I scream with pain.

The announcer says, "I think Meadowlark is badly hurt. He needs a nurse."

"Oh, no," I yell. "I need two nurses!"

All my teammates gather round. One massages my arm. Another yells, "What wrong, Lemon? Your arm hurt?"

"No," I cry. "It's my leg."

We laugh over that one as I substitute a ball with a long elastic string for the one I brought off the court.

I take the ball under my arm and jog back onto the court for the foul shot. Players line up on either side, and the suspense grows. I bounce the ball a few times and then let it sail toward the basket.

The ball goes way above the rim. Oops! It halts in midair and magically returns to me. Kids scream in surprise.

I throw the ball to the referee. It comes back to me before it gets to him.

I toss it to a fan in the stands. Woman, child, or man—they all forget the ball has elastic on it in the excitement of the moment. They scream or jump out of the way.

Instantly, the ball comes back to me. Everyone has a big laugh at the trick.

Everyone except the ref who orders me, "Get that ball off the court!"

I dutifully obey and return with a ball that's weighted on one side, which makes the ball wobble all around—sideways, zigzag, any way but straight.

The ball wobbles toward the basket. "What kind of ball is that?" the referee screams. "Get it out of here!"

The next ball looks beautiful. Just to be sure, the referee grabs it. Swooosh! The ball flattens in his hands, the air escapes through a few holes in the hide.

Now the referee's really furious. He goes and gets a ball himself. He bounces it hard on the floor, he's so mad, and the ball soars high over his head. All the players on the sidelines throw towels in the air and double over with laughter.

People see these gags year after year and still enjoy them.

My smile was really important in foreign countries where I often had to pantomime the jokes because I couldn't speak the language. My smile was the door opener. I'd giggle. I'd laugh. I'd cavort. I'd high-step. I'd cackle.

Lots of kids have thought I'm a big toy. "Can we take Meadowlark home so I can play with him?" they ask their mothers.

As I developed as a clown, I learned to read crowds from the minute we hit the floor, and I made it my business to whip them up. If they were high when we started, I wanted them exhausted by the time we left. If they were quiet, I wanted to endear them to us and open them up as soon as possible. I felt loose and funny and good about myself, and I'd mug, make faces, giggle, laugh, whatever. If an opponent was on the free-throw line, I might laugh just as he was shooting.

If a woman stood to leave, I'd stop dribbling, look up at her, and shout, "Where you goin', lady?" If that caused her to laugh, I'd follow up quickly, "What you laughin' at, lady?" I might just point and taunt and tease in a singsong voice, "We know where you're goin'!"

I've done five minutes on a man dropping a bag of popcorn. "I'm glad you're not on my team! Pick 'em all up, right now! You missed one! Don't eat 'em! They're fuzzy! Maybe your mom can feed you next time, sir!"

My game grew along with my comedy. If an opponent tried to stop the comedy show, we'd blow him out with basketball. If the other team sagged in on the pivot man and kept him from running the routines, a Bobby Joe Mason, a Curly Neal, or a Clarence Wilson would shoot their lights out.

These men, and many others like them, came out of colleges and universities where they had been all-Americans with high shooting percentages. They might shoot 10 of 10 on a given night, and when the opposition realized there was no future in double- or triple-teaming me in the pivot, we would go back to our fun.

If a man stopped me from going to my right for a funny move, I'd go to my left. It might not be quite as funny, but I'd score. I once was covered so well that I slipped trying to shoot past my man. From the floor I flipped the ball up between his legs and scored. It became part of my bag of tricks. A man might stop me to the right; he might even stop me to the left; but he's not going to stop me from being funny.

I couldn't believe the applause, the laughter. It was almost physical, lifting me, inspiring me, warming me. I couldn't get enough of it. Every night I could hardly wait to charge from the locker room into the gym to get another fix of crowd reaction.

Lots of things went wrong in my life and career, and somehow things were never really the same after the original team I joined started to break up and be replaced by new faces. You've got to understand that when a man plays more than seven thousand games for the same team for more than twenty years, he winds up playing with a lot of different people.

My favorite team was the first group I traveled with on the big squad. Over the years, though, we have had some outstanding players to make up an all-star Globetrotter squad. Until I saw Wilt Chamberlain play, I thought the best basketball player ever was Donald Byrd out of Cleveland. He was big and strong and fast, a good ballhandler, a good shooter from anywhere on the floor, and he could rebound and play defense. Complete.

Wilt's the best, of course. I've heard all the arguments about Bill Russell, Magic Johnson, Larry Bird, Kareem Abdul-Jabbar, Jerry West, Oscar Robertson, Elgin Baylor. These are all players I admire. I would have loved to have played with them or against them.

Connie Hawkins was a player from the streets of New York who had as much talent in his little finger as a whole team and who could have been the best ever, Trotter, NBAer, whatever. His career was interrupted by legal complications, and age may have caught up with him, but then I didn't think he ever respected his own talent enough either. Other than Chamberlain, Hawkins was probably the most naturally gifted athlete I've ever seen on the court.

None was better than Wilt. He played with the Globetrotters before going to the NBA, signing for a bonus as big as my salary and a salary of sixty-five thousand dollars on top of that. The man could score at will. He was the most dominating force the game has ever seen, and all the statistics bear that out. He was bigger than life off the court, too.

I was assigned to teach Wilt the ropes, show him how we do things, and watch out for him. He was young and naive at first, but that didn't last long. When he and I went nightclubbing, no one looked at me. They looked at the seven-footer with the wads of bills in his pockets. Even after he made the NBA, he played summers in Europe for us for big dollars. Imagine being the biggest, richest, most famous man on an entire continent!

He and I squabbled and argued, but stories you hear about my attacking him or fighting him are pure fiction. I may have been a fool at times in my life, but I was never crazy enough to take on a man who was seven one and weighed 275 pounds. He was a mountain and strong enough to handle anyone. One time, as a gag, he grabbed me by the shirt and pinned me up against the wall, two feet off the ground. I was six two and 190 then.

Wilt was sure a fun guy to travel and party with. He was with us when we visited the Soviet Union during the Khrushchev regime.

Abe always wanted to be the first at everything. No American team had ever played basketball in Russia, so even though the terms weren't so good, Abe accepted the Russian offer. They couldn't pay us in American dollars, and Russian money wasn't good outside their country, so they promised to pay Abe in Russian sable and other furs. Once we got to Russia, the fur offer was rescinded, and I think Abe was paid in Russian stamps. Not the rarest, by far, but Abe wasn't a stamp collector so he didn't know the difference.

We played nine games in seven days near the Kremlin in a Moscow arena that held sixteen thousand. The place was sold out for every game, but the first three nights nobody laughed at anything. It was eerie. We did everything we could think of to open them up.

I fell down and shot a hook shot, and it went in. Still, no reaction. I lay on the floor and shot two more in. Still, no laughter. It wasn't until I went into the stands during the fourth game and started shaking hands that people began to smile, then to laugh. I think it was a totally new experience for them. Once they started laughing, the joint was jumping.

The Russians arranged everything for us, including tours, which we had to go on. One day we were told we were going to the Russian library near Red Square. We never got that far.

Wilt and I had our eye on a cannon in front of the library that looked as big as a house, and we wanted to check it out. We were intercepted by the guide and led back to our group. We soon found out why.

Three black limousines pulled up and Nikita Khrushchev himself stepped out and greeted us. He was a short man who could speak a few words of English.

"You an American?" he asked me.

I thought, *What else could I be? Where could all these tall black guys come from, anyway?* But, of course, I merely answered yes.

We exchanged a few other words, and I thought, *What an honor to be talking to a man with such power.*

really nice little man. I was honored to be talking to a man with such power.

All of a sudden the cameras came out, and we realized that the meeting was a setup. I looked around and saw security people on the roofs of all the buildings.

Immediately, other tourists and people on the square gathered around, and I wound up at the back of the crowd. A year later when Khrushchev came to America, I realized how wrong a first impression can be. He'd been so cordial that day on Red Square. Could that have been the same man who pounded his shoe on the podium at the United Nations and screamed, "We will bury you!"?

22

The Sadness Behind the Grin

The clown prince made everybody laugh and forget their problems—everybody but himself and his own family. There have been drawbacks to the life of a celebrity, but none so great as the loss of my marriage.

While I was basically enjoying the life of a celebrity—despite the exhaustion of midnight travel and two games in one day—my being on the road so long was too much for Willye, almost from the very beginning. Every time I left she looked at me as if she wanted a promise that this would be the last time. Yet Willye knew I had to keep the one job I had, the only one I had ever wanted, if we wanted a good life for the family. In our ignorance, we thought a good life meant a nice house, private school educations for our kids, running in the right circles, wearing the right clothes, going to the best restaurants, driving the right cars. But Willye didn't like the fact that it was so hard.

Together Willye and I had celebrated my success as lead clown in Yankee Stadium in the summer of 1958. Together we rejoiced over the birth of our daughter, Beverly, that same summer. And we shouted for joy when I returned the next season to learn that the position of lead clown was mine.

That year almost everything seemed to go our way. We had moved from our duplex on Pearl Harbor Street to the attorney's house Willye had, at first, been so skeptical about, a five-bedroom home with lots of land and trees in Fairfield. That was a long way from our original flat on Railroad Avenue, where the roar of the elevated train passing by boomed through our living room.

But the next summer the gap between our outward success and our actual financial position became all too evident to us. I was the lead clown for the Harlem Globetrotters, but my salary was not enough to pay the first and second mortgages on our home, another loan, and several other bills. I wanted to get a summer job to help make ends meet, but Abe asked me not to work so I would be good and rested for the next season. I told him I didn't think I could make it financially. He told me if I would agree not to work, he'd send me some money that I could pay back the next season. I agreed. He sent two hundred dollars. It didn't last long.

I thought about giving up my dream, but it was what I had always wanted, and I enjoyed it. Plus, I didn't know where I could earn more money. The Globetrotters weren't well paid compared to other athletes, but we earned salaries way beyond our black brothers in the ghettos of America.

Willye and I were down to enough food in the house for one more meal, I had fifteen dollars, and the mortgage was due. We were on each other's backs. I had to do something. I tried not to panic, but I did do something foolish. When some buddies invited me to play poker with them, I took my last fifteen dollars and said yes. I waited until the banks closed, then I hit on an older woman who did domestic work in our area. "Mattie, I'm embarrassed. The banks just closed on me, and I need fifty bucks, just till Monday. I'm good for it."

"Oh, child, you know I would lend you everything I had if it was a thousand, but all I got is fifteen dollars and it's my phone bill money, due next week. If you goin' pay it back Monday, you can have it."

"You got it, Mattie. And thanks."

I walked into the poker game with thirty dollars and an empty checkbook. The first thing my buddies said was that they hoped I brought the deed to my house. " 'Cause we goin' take you for everything you got." We all laughed, but my laugh was hollow. I knew I had to be good that night, because there would be no second chance. I could throw my house deed and my marriage certificate on the table if I went broke, because neither would be worth a dime by then.

When I arrived home at 4:00 A.M., Willye was sitting in the

living room, her eyes red, her mouth tight. We're talkin' MAD. "Would you believe I was working all night, trying to raise the mortgage money?"

"No." Icicles hung from her lips.

When I laid six hundred dollars on the table, she thawed. I paid back my debt, set aside enough for the mortgage, bought food, and saved a hundred. Next afternoon came the call I knew would come. The poker players wanted a rematch. I shouldn't have done it. It was a long shot.

Would you believe I won another five hundred? I lived up to the reputation of that gambler's gambler, Meadow Lemon II, my dad. From his experience, I knew I couldn't support myself playing poker, but I also decided that my family would never be in danger of going hungry again.

In the next years, my salary increased to twenty thousand dollars a year. We put our children—George, Beverly, Donna, Robin, and Jonathan—in private schools so they could receive a good education, just as Willye and I had dreamed. Willye bought them clothes as classy as those of their schoolmates who were the sons and daughters of white professionals.

After all, I was the clown prince of the Harlem Globetrotters; our children deserved the best. Yet Willye and I were living way beyond our means, and no one knew it better than the bill collectors who pursued me. And the two of us. We fought constantly over the phone about finances. The more we spent, the more pressure I felt. There was more to this American dream, it seemed, than just a nice home and running in the right circles. But what was it? Neither of us seemed to know.

And we weren't together much to discuss our problems and try to work them out. I had tried to see Willye more than the Trotters' incredible schedule allowed (many seasons, 320 games in about ten months). Once she came to England to meet me for a vacation, another time to Germany, but these trips came out of my own pocket. I traveled around the world to places millionaires visited, but I myself was making a salary of twenty thousand dollars in the early 1960s, and forty thousand dollars by the late 1960s. More than that, both of us felt our five kids needed one parent at home most of the time.

I was driven to hold onto my dream. And yet I knew I should spend more time with my family. When our games were on the East Coast, this was possible. New England, after all, is a small area. If I had a game in Buffalo, New York, I left after the game at about eleven o'clock, drove most of the night, and arrived home at four in the morning, slept a while, and then got up. If it was Saturday, I saw the kids. If not, they were gone to school. Usually I had to leave after lunch to drive back to upstate New York to meet the team for that night's game. A merry-go-round, it was. But without the fun.

I think even Willye will agree that I was a good father when I was home. The kids and I got along real well, and I was the type who helped out around the house. Beverly wrote in a paper for elementary school that her daddy's job was washing dishes! It was the only thing she had seen me do during the time I was home.

Robin once told her teacher that I lived at the airport, because that's where they drove me when I went back on the road. She thought I was a visitor.

Kids are cuddly. They say funny things. But to think my daughters thought I was a dishwasher who lived at the airport!

Constantly upset with each other and only occasionally harmonious, Willye and I started justifying things we might not have justified otherwise. I began spending more evenings at nightclubs with the boys. And the girls. The combination is inevitable. If you were at the clubs in the evenings, the girls were available. Women hung around the team.

Nearly everybody on the road slept with someone different every night. It wasn't hidden. It wasn't shocking. It was simply something that went with road life. You had to be careful if you tried to sneak someone into the hotel, but most of the guys went clubbing, picked up a woman, entertained her at her place, and then came back to the hotel alone. Men back in Wilmington had slept with other women behind their wives' backs or lived with different common-law wives. There was really nothing wrong with it, I rationalized. It was simply a part of marriage—I thought.

The guys on the Trotters who didn't do that were not cool. They were square. Religious. But they weren't part of the "in" crowd. And that's what I began to enjoy. I hid my womanizing from my wife—or thought I had—to spare her feelings and spare me her wrath, but to me it became a way of life.

Finally, in the last couple of years of our marriage, it was apparent to both Willye and me that we should move away from each other. I began finding reasons not to come home at the end of the season. If the Trotters had something for me to do promotionally, I'd jump at the chance. Again I felt homeless. Unloved. And I looked for companionship everywhere I could.

I became addicted. I saw a skirt, a shapely form, a smile, a look, and I wanted it. We played ball during the day and the early evening, and we slept with women at night. I had a rule I thought was moral. I would never come on to another man's wife. Single girls, however, were fair game. I don't like to admit that, and I'm not proud of it. It sickens me to think back on it and how low I had fallen, especially when I realize how calloused I was toward it then.

But I can't deny it. No one can change, as I have, unless the person finally admits his sins. It would take a couple of painful years for me and my family before I would own up to them.

23

Squabbles, Strikes,
and Suspensions

Unfortunately, I have to admit it. I ran around on my wife, and I was also greedy. I was always waiting for that big financial break. I was addicted to the applause and the admiration of the crowd. I wanted it all, and I wanted it now.

I was still having some fun, though the search for more and more fulfillment was leaving me empty. If I had a problem, I would solve it with things. I played whist, a game like bridge, gambled, played poker, went to nightclubs, and looked for women. I wasn't happy at home, and I looked to pleasure to fill the void.

I was also egotistical. I didn't know any better or any different. I had wanted to be a Globetrotter all my life, and now I was the one name that came to mind when people mentioned that team. I had it all, and it wasn't enough.

It wasn't that I never tried to help the new guys, even the ones who were after my job. I enjoyed helping out, coaching, tutoring, bringing guys along. I worked with Curly Neal and Gator Rivers on their dribbling and with Geese Ausbie on his showmanship, yet soon I was told to leave this to the coaches.

The coach at that time told me, "Now, Meadowlark, that's my job, not yours."

I saw tremendous potential in a ballplayer named Bobby Hunter. But when I spent a little extra time with him, I was told—

by everyone but him—to back off. Apparently, that was also a threat.

It bothered me when new players tried to take a reem that I had made popular and use it when I was on the floor. I was vocal about that. Some took it as possessiveness or protection of my role.

I wasn't jealous. I was unique. Timing was an asset, a trademark. It didn't pay to upstage the lead clown after I had put in so much time working on my craft, perfecting every expression, every nuance. I had learned my role from road managers Ducky Moore and Parnell Woods, coaches Duke Cumberland and Pop Gates, and the showmen who came before me. Sam Wheeler showed me how to move the ball like it was a hot potato and to hold it like it was a soft-boiled egg.

In the old days, the veterans were like coaches, and I took advantage of that, learning all I could. But the new players wanted to be great all at once without investing time in the trenches.

When Abe Saperstein died in 1966, a lot of basketball history died with him. He had put the Trotters on the card with NBA games to help draw crowds and increase interest in the fledgling league. At the same time he was part owner of the Philadelphia NBA entry. When his relationship with the NBA went sour and he was blackballed, he started the American Basketball Association and put us on the cards with that league. Sometimes players would graduate from the Globetrotters to the ABA and wind up playing for the same owner.

Abe's attorney decided to sell the Trotters in 1967 for the sake of the family. Metromedia bid against a Chicago group made up of a young man named George Gillette and the Palmer family of the Palmer Hotels. Gillette, Potter Palmer, and John O'Neil of Miami, Florida, bought the club for $3.71 million, and a new era began.

I went in before the season to negotiate my salary, and I wasn't any more successful than I had ever been. I was woefully underpaid compared to NBA players who played one-fourth the number of games and had all kinds of other benefits. But I proved I wasn't a businessman or a negotiator when all I could get out of the new ownership was a small cost-of-living raise. It was a good living, but nothing like it should have been.

When the team was touring Europe, Gillette and Palmer came

to look us over. They chatted with us at a gala party in Rome, and we didn't see them again for the whole season. They were nice young guys who were good businessmen, but it was clear to me they didn't understand the game of basketball.

The next time I ran into them, in 1971, it was also in Italy but under less than happy circumstances. My marriage was on the rocks, and side businesses I had attempted were losing money. I put all that aside and was still able to do my show, but while I was playing on a soccer field in Torino, a squabble got out of hand. A couple of my comedic tricks made an opponent feel humiliated, and he told me not to do it again. To me, he seemed unusually touchy.

The next time up the court, I shot between his legs. He shoved me.

Frustrated, at odds with the world, I felt the way I had in the army just after my father died. I glared at him. "You're crazy, man. If you can't take it, you shouldn't be playing." We traded words throughout the first two quarters, and at half time we were still jawing as we headed to the locker room, drinking Cokes and threatening each other. A teammate of his grabbed me and held me so the guy could punch me out. They were both bigger than I was. My mind raced back to my childhood when Titty Boo had beaten me up.

I frantically shook free and grabbed a pop bottle. I swung wildly, hitting one with the bottle but winding up on the ground by the time the rest of the players from both teams arrived and broke it up. I finished the game, but when I saw the guy later, I thought about hitting him. I restrained myself, though.

The opponents said they wouldn't play against me anymore, and that brought our owners flying in from the States. I wasn't asked my version of the story, but I was suspended by George Gillette with no defense. He asked, "Will you be prepared to join the team in Allentown, Pennsylvania, when we get back?"

I thought about that one. "I don't think so."

"What do you mean?"

"If you're going to suspend me, you might as well suspend me for good." There were only three weeks left on the European tour.

I waited in the lobby of the hotel while George talked to the rest of the team. They told him that if they had to play without me, they wanted more money. He said that if that was the way it had to be, he would cancel the rest of the trip. The team walked out on him.

Curly Neal, the bald dribbler who is a dear friend, a great shooter, and one of my favorite showmen, came to me in the lobby. "Let's go home."

Gillette rushed to me. "What's happening? What's wrong with this team? Talk to them, Meadowlark. Do it for me."

"How can I? I'm suspended."

Something about my hard-nosed attitude appealed to George, and we became friends after that. The walkout was averted. The guy who attacked me wound up suing me. I paid him off to get rid of him and learned that fists only get you in trouble. I wasn't learning much else, though. Nothing was working for me. The crowds thought I was the clown prince, the laughing, cavorting showman who loved the game and life. I loved the game, but life you could have.

The following season we did a TV special in Atlantic City, and our guest star was Soupy Sales. He came into the gym and someone tossed him a ball. He threw up a shot from half-court, and it swished. He looked shocked, and we all laughed, someone betting him a million he couldn't do it again as long as he lived. The ball went back to Soupy. Up went the shot. In! I doubt he ever got his million, but I started to wonder if he had hustled us. Maybe this was a guy who had been practicing that shot the way I had practiced hook shots all my life.

When we went to taping, we found out he had indeed been lucky. He couldn't buy a shot for miles and miles of video tape. We all got quite a kick out of it, and he and I really hit it off. Later he introduced me to Stan Greeson, his manager.

When Nate Branch, a young Trotter who liked to sing as much as I did, and I started a little nightclub act, we signed Stan on as our manager. Not much came of it—in fact, Nate and I had a falling out that was never really healed—but Stan wound up being the agent I had always needed.

He got me a good contract and a decent salary, and I thought things had turned for the better. The problem was, there was discord on the team, my personal and business life was in shambles, and the solution I dreamed up was the worst possible cure. I tried to get into the clothing business on the side. But I spent too much on the incidentals, like office space and furniture, and I couldn't devote enough time to the business. I went into debt, refinanced my house, started a new company, and failed again. At least I had scruples. Rather than declaring bankruptcy, I got out of the business and set up a plan where I could pay off all the creditors.

When the problems between management and the team reached a boiling point in 1971, I was glad I had Stan as my agent. The thing most of the other players didn't realize, however, is that I would have gone on strike with them if they'd asked. Leon Hillard was behind the strike, which took place before a game at the McMorran Sports Arena in Port Huron, Michigan. He had had problems with me in the past, thought I was a friend of management, and so had all the strike meetings without me.

I thought the concerns of the players were valid. They wanted better working conditions, an easier travel schedule and, of course, more money. Frank Stephens, a six-year man, served as spokesman. He told the press, "We just want decent salaries, a pension plan, a better insurance plan, meal money. We want to be treated as men and given our human dignity."

They complained of the crowded team bus and of the low salaries. The average was supposed to be around $20,000 a year, but my $40,000 brought that average up. The minimum for a rookie was $7,800, compared to more than twice that in the National Basketball Association at that time.

When the team struck, however, I wasn't invited, and I wasn't involved. Once they began to get more demanding and ask for more than they had in the beginning, I was glad I wasn't part of it. I was threatened by former teammates, put down by their representatives, called a fool by some, an Uncle Tom by others.

That's one thing I've never been, in spite of the number of people who said so. There are even former Trotters who said they felt like Uncle Toms, cavorting on the court for the white man, looking stupid, playing dumb. My answer to that is that no one made us play for the Harlem Globetrotters. And we entertained fans of all races. I was aware of the prejudice, sure. You'd have had to be blind and deaf not to be aware of it. But there were also incidents that went beyond race.

I remember the time when we played an all-black team before an all-white crowd, and when we went to the bus station, we had to eat at a black-only diner in the back. A man came to me outside carrying his beautiful blonde daughter of about six. She wanted to meet me, to give me a hug and a kiss. She said, "I just love you, Meadowlark!"

Her eyes shone, and her smile was radiant. She leaped from her father's arms to mine and squeezed me tight. I laughed. "Well, thank you, sweetheart. That's nice."

The man's eyes were moist. With her cheek at my ear, he leaned close to the other. "Thank you, Meadowlark. She's dying."

It was all I could do to hang on to her. My strength seeped away. I held her close so she couldn't see me crying.

"Thank you, thank you, Meadowlark," the little girl said. "You're so funny, and I love you and wish I could take you home with me!"

I choked. "I do, too, honey." She was too young to see color.

And then there was the time I heard a little boy cackling at courtside. He just screamed and hollered and giggled as if he had never seen anything so funny in his life. And he kept calling, "Meadowlark Lemon! Meadowlark Lemon!" When the ball went out of bounds, the man next to him gathered it up and tossed it to me. I lobbed a pass toward the boy. It hit him in the chest and rolled back to me.

I have used this bit all over the world, tossing the ball back and forth with whoever throws it in. They don't know what to do with it, and it brings down the house. I've done it with cops, soldiers, women, old men, kids, whoever. (I got arrested in a Communist country once because I did it with a cop and they thought I was making fun of authority!)

When the ball came back, I tossed it to the boy again. Again, it hit him and rolled back. One more time it happened. The crowd loved it, but I wondered what was going on. The man next to him told me by mouthing the words. "He's blind."

I took the ball to the boy and helped him hold it. He threw it back. I gave him a hug and heard him calling my name and cheering the rest of the game. He couldn't see color either.

So, no, I wouldn't have struck because I felt like an Uncle Tom. I didn't. I would have struck to support the demands of the whole team, but when they chose to leave me out, I chose to stay out.

They said I would look like a fool to stay out of the strike, but I was hurt. They thought I got privileged treatment, a higher salary, more TV appearances, stuff like that. They were right, and maybe I was getting bigheaded. But when they finally needed me, they didn't have me.

24

Unraveling

Management courted me during the strike. They wanted to know what to do, how bad things were, how to fix them, and how deeply the feelings went.

I was honest. I told them that the guys had some gripes that were valid and some that weren't. The fact is, everybody but the striking players realized that I was the key because of my team position. I'm not trying to brag, but people who know show business will tell you that you can put a whole new cast of characters around the leading man, and the audience won't know the difference.

You could change the cast in *The King and I*, and as long as Yul Brenner was in there, everyone was happy. Now that he's gone, I think that show will fade. Every star playing the king will be compared to the man who defined the role. And how about the Rolling Stones? Only the real fan knows the back-up players. Mick Jagger and four others, within reason, would still be the Stones.

It wasn't helping my humility any to think that management could field a new team, as long as I was there, and they wouldn't suffer from the strike. My agent, Stan Greeson, got involved, worked out an attractive deal for me, got me more control, and allowed me to bring back Marques Haynes and the players we wanted to build around. Suddenly, we were back in business.

Marques and I coached two units and kept in touch daily. Some of the strikers got hurt bad, but I felt Marques and I were the best things that had happened to the organization in years. I became more and more important to the package, and my salary kept increasing. Finally, I was making high-income-bracket dollars. The NBA was still way ahead of me, however, and that would start gnawing at me because of my greed. I wasn't getting any younger, but I was expected to do an awful lot for the club.

We were still playing three hundred games a year. I was in charge of coaching, conditioning, choosing players, keeping track of them on the road and, hardly least, playing as the star clown. I enjoyed it in many ways, but it was exhausting. I was flown to different cities for appearances, and I started being driven to games rather than taking the bus. Players resented my popularity and my style, which I can see now was getting overbearing.

I felt I had paid my dues and deserved every good thing I got. I also felt I deserved more. Maybe I took a little lesson from Abe without knowing it. If a young player was properly respectful, he had all of my time and interest he wanted. Anyone who wanted more than I thought was necessary to keep him happy went away disappointed.

I sensed myself losing the respect of the team, and I reacted by becoming more distant. On the court, I was still the wild funny man. Off the court, I had few friends.

My players thought I was a relic, an egotistical, aloof know-it-all. I probably was. I thought my ballplayers were babies. They had training rooms and trainers and whirlpools and rubdowns and taping of the ankles before every game. I was from the old school where if you sprained your ankle, you just laced your sneaker up tighter and hobbled around until the pain passed. It seemed to me we were injured a lot less frequently when we didn't have paid personnel to watch out for us. No one would admit to pain or take himself out of a game unless he wanted to lose his spot to someone else. I played more than 7,500 *consecutive* games, something unheard of today.

I only missed two games in more than twenty years, and I was late only two times. After I had played my first two hundred games, I was so sick in Cologne, Germany, that I passed out at a restaurant, headfirst into my soup. I missed that game, and though I was ready the next night, I was told to sit out one more.

It's fair to say I wasn't sympathetic to the modern pansy who couldn't play with pain. My high-school football coach, Mr. Robinson, had told it to me straight: "Everybody gets hurt sometime. If you're not ever hurt, you're not doing your job." I told my team of the time I broke my finger during a game, set it myself on the way up the court, taped it later, and didn't miss a minute.

My philosophy was that we could never settle for mediocrity. There was no option but excellence. I hated to tell kids when they hadn't made the team, but I was looking for guys who could fake so good that the whole building leaned the wrong way when they went up for a shot.

The players may have thought that I was a good showman, but they didn't think I was fun to work for. They didn't realize that a player-coach can't see all the shots. It was impossible for me to slap each player on the back and praise him right away. In fact, in my early Trotter days, we might knock a player down a peg by smiling at him and saying, "You didn't do nothin' but your job, brother."

After the game we might compliment each other for "a decent game" or "a good job." But playing excellent basketball and being hilarious, that was what we were paid to do.

I wasn't any more pleasant an employee than I was an employer. I didn't allow management to interfere with the game because most of them didn't know what they were talking about. If they tried, I could be downright nasty. "If you put me in charge, let me be in charge," I told them.

Somewhere over the years, I had evolved from a naive, fun-loving entertainer to a moody, withdrawn guy who was the direct opposite of what I was on the court. I pretended to be self-confident and content. Inside I was depressed and scared. I didn't know where this life was leading me. Lots of kids were coming into the organization, and they seemed younger every year. We had little in common, including styles of playing.

It wasn't that I didn't still do the occasional good deed, or that I didn't still care about my hometown. My pride made me angry that Wilmington had brought back Althea Gibson, Roman Gabriel, and Sonny Jurgenson for their special days, but I had never been invited back. I thought I was a bigger star, more well known, yet there had never been a Meadowlark Lemon Day.

But I have to say that once Wilmington got started on it, they did it up right, made me feel welcome, admitted it was overdue, and made it a beautiful day in March of 1971. The city was torn apart from racial unrest, so the timing was crucial. Desegregation had finally come to the town, but rather than busing white kids into the black school, the burden seemed to fall totally on the blacks to go out of their way to integrate the white school.

As long as Williston Industrial was the black school and New Hanover High was the white school, just as they had been when I was in high school, things were tense but stable for years. When the school board reacted to the desegregation order by turning Williston into a junior high and integrating New Hanover, it was more than the blacks could take. They felt used and abused, and they let people know about it. Some of the students and a couple of former students became what was known as the Wilmington 10. They boycotted the new school, and violence erupted. Shots were fired, people wounded, two killed, stores burned, businesses looted.

That was the situation I walked into for Meadowlark Lemon Day. Mr. Bess, Mr. Haynes, Earl Jackson, Coaches Robinson and Corbin, my mother, my wife, and several other VIP's were on hand. I visited the schools, gave some basketball demonstrations, heard a lot of speeches, gave a few, and was made an honorary member of the board of directors of the Boys' Club.

I pleaded with everyone, black and white, to work to keep the schools open for the sake of the children. "Get the education. Stay in school. Let's get things together and get this trouble over." I knew things were bad, but I didn't realize they would get much worse and that I would play a larger role in the crisis a few months later.

I was especially happy about getting on the board of the Boys' Club, even honorarily, because Mr. Bess was near retirement, and I wanted to see Earl get the top job. He had put in the years and given of himself, way above and beyond the call of duty.

When the new president of the Boys' Club was named, he was a younger and more educated man. I was mad, and I let it be known. My recommendation had been ignored, and in my opinion, Earl was slighted. I didn't think he should take it.

I looked around the country and put the finger on a friend in Las Vegas who had a similar job available for twice the salary. Earl's wife was a nurse and could find work anywhere. I couldn't wait to drop the news on him. "Earl, this is your chance to show 'em and to make yourself some decent money doing what you do best and doing what you like to do."

He thought about it a long time. The decision he came to was difficult. "Meadowlark, I appreciate you and what you're tryin' to do for me. I may be a fool to turn it down, but I can't leave these kids. They need me."

Though I had visited and given some basketball demonstrations, the Globetrotters had never played in my hometown. We scheduled a game in the newly desegregated high-school gym two months later, right in the middle of the violence over the Wilmington 10. Things were so bad that it appeared the game would be canceled.

Whites seemed to blame the entire conflict on the blacks. Blacks were outraged that only blacks had been arrested. The jury was made up of mostly blacks, and the prosecuting attorney was pushing for a mistrial. He claimed he was sick and wanted a delay, but he was accused of wanting a jury that wouldn't be so clearly weighted in favor of the blacks. Schools were shut down, curfews imposed. The racial tension was at a boiling point, and a solution had to be found.

Leaders of the community asked me to help, and the Pepsi-Cola Company assigned a pilot and a company jet to fly me into the city every day for about five days before the game. I was afraid each time I flew in there. Dick Gregory had been shot when he tried to help settle the riots in the Watts area of Los Angeles. I could also run into a stray bullet.

Again I urged calm to both blacks and whites. Some resisted my appeals. They tried to tell me that I had been gone too long, and that I didn't understand. I understood. It was still my town, and I wanted access to the people via radio and television. Before I went on I was counseled what to say and what not to say. I refused to be anyone's spokesman. "Sorry, man, but I got to say what I got to say, and I will."

I told the people that the world was watching. I told whites they were being irresponsible and blacks they were shortsighted. "You can ruin this town or build it back up."

I asked that the schools that had been closed until I arrived be opened so I could come talk to the students. "You have to be an example to the older generation. You're the future. If you want there to be a Wilmington, North Carolina, ten years from now, you've got to lead the way. We're gonna have a ball game, and the crowd will be mixed. . . . So will the players. The Trotter team is black, the opposition is mixed.

"We're coming because we love you, and we want to have fun. Let's show the world what can happen when people think rationally."

I had been around the world several times. I had entertained kings and presidents. I was more articulate than when I left. Some were suspicious of that. The local police and the national guard predicted a major uprising at the game. They said my efforts would fail. I pleaded with them to be prepared if they had to but to stay outside the school unless they were needed.

The game went off without a hitch. No threats, no staring down. Blacks and whites sat together, laughed together, sang together. I felt it was one of the best things I ever accomplished.

Meanwhile, my agent had done such a good job for me and as a sort of unofficial mediator between the players and management during the strike that the Globetrotter owners made him president of the club. I suppose still retaining him as my agent was a conflict of interest, but he was a friend and we trusted each other. My role on the team continued to grow.

And my marriage continued to crumble. I was home less and less. When Willye and I talked on the phone, it was only to argue. I talked to the kids a lot, but it was clear they were hearing only her side of the story and I was coming out the bad guy. I felt terribly offended.

The team changed hands yet again with Metromedia finally buying it. They put a promotion man on the road who actually tried to get into our act one night by taking over the microphone and attempting to be funny. I went after him right then. The crowd thought it was all part of the gag, but he knew he'd done wrong. And he knew I seriously wanted a piece of him. He ran from the arena and flew to Metromedia headquarters in Los Angeles.

By now my pay was more than $100,000 a year, and I was trying to parlay it into bigger dollars. Marques Haynes and I started a very short-lived promotional business out of New York, but it fell apart. More money lost.

I kept resolving to quit going after the big financial score. I should have learned by then who I could trust and who I couldn't. But I had myself overrated. I had accomplished the great American dream. I was living proof that a man can do anything he really wants to do if he invests the time.

I learned slowly that you get only one miracle like that per lifetime. I wanted my whole life to be that way: Any woman I took a fancy to was going to give me the high of the century. The next time I called home, my kids would love me and my wife would think I was great and all that would be healed in an instant. I would make a small investment that would result in millions coming into my bank account. My next friend would be true blue. My next raise would make me the highest paid athlete in history. My expectations were set so high that I could only fail, only be disappointed.

By the late 1970s, Willye and I had been arguing and fighting for so long that we were enemies who happened to be married. I was dating two other women, and Willye had had enough. She once told me in the heat of an argument, "Someday you're going to die just like your father did."

The kids were suffering, scared, wondering what was going to happen to the family. George stuck with me, but the rest wrote me off, at least during that time. One even helped her mother get a lawyer.

I had to go home after one road trip. There were too many things that needed to be done, and it would have been worse than irresponsible to stay away, much as I wanted to. I let my new woman off at her place in New York, then drove to Bridgeport. It was like walking into a meat locker. I could have left my coat on. I tried to get my business in order and help out around the house where I could. I felt sadness and impending doom. Willye and I had had a lot of years together, some of the early ones very warm and happy and full of memories. The kids were the most important people in the world to each of us. I hated what was happening, but I was riding the rapids toward the falls.

The next day a sheriff's deputy came to the door. He had a summons for one Meadow George Lemon III. A major change was in the wind.

25

Stabbed in the Back

My wife had me thrown out of my own home, and all I felt was relief. I hurriedly packed a few things, felt my wife's icy stare, and jumped into my black cherry Lincoln. I was about fifteen minutes down Route 95 before I realized I had nowhere to go.

What else was new? Meadow Lemon had no home. I'd never really had a home, even when Willye and I moved into our first house. I was there so little that it was just a resting place between seasons and road trips.

I called my friend, Hy Lit, a popular disc jockey, who was almost as well-known as Dick Clark of "American Bandstand." He set me up in the penthouse of an Atlantic City hotel for just thirty-five dollars a night during the slow season. I was in fat city for a while, enjoying myself and my freedom. I thought that now I could really get my head together and do some serious thinking. All I wound up doing was playing, having fun, and getting little accomplished except trying to plan bigger and better schemes for myself.

I had recently signed a multiyear deal at $225,000 a year that kept me the highest paid Trotter ever. I felt good about that, and I was looking for a good investment, maybe something that would showcase my other talents: acting, singing, business (see how slow I learned?). Wilt Chamberlain and I had talked about starting a comedy basketball team. I really thought we could do it someday.

The divorce case was long and messy, and in the meantime I

had to get back on the road with the team. It was a crazy, mixed-up year with everything falling in on me. The team was suspicious and wary of me. My wife wanted a settlement. I was not a happy person.

Still, the termination of that marriage, I thought, was something to look forward to. I didn't realize that it was like an expected death. When people know an elderly loved one is about to die, and when they also agree that it would only be for the best, they are sometimes surprised by how deeply shocked and hurt they are when it finally happens. It was that way with me.

I had a four-hour drive after I dropped off my attorney following the final decree. It was the longest drive of my life. I expected to feel free, relieved, happy, to a greater degree than I had when we were officially separated. The opposite happened. For some reason, anger and bitterness rose in my throat. I was melancholy about the memories, and it seemed all I could dredge up were the happy ones.

Willye had been my teen-age sweetheart. There had been a lot of love between us. What had gone wrong? Could the kids survive it? Would they hate me forever? I didn't want to go back and make it work. That was out of the question. I'm not sure Willye felt that way. In fact, I think she has never forgiven me for leaving, even though she sent me away. I think she really wanted me to fight the summons, fight the divorce, and try to win her back. Maybe she was more of a romantic than I was.

I felt like someone had stripped a warm fur coat off me in the middle of a blizzard. I was lost. I had friends, even two lady friends. My mother was still in New York. I was well paid, well recognized, and was living in the fast lane. Yet everything I had ever wanted to be right was wrong. I was a failure, and I couldn't shake that feeling.

At times I felt I was right and everyone else was wrong, but down deep I knew it wasn't true. I wasn't without merit. I was a hard worker, dedicated to my craft and to excellence. But the bottom line was that I was dedicated to Meadowlark Lemon, and I didn't feel worthy of that dedication.

I hated myself and the place I'd brought myself. Something inside told me that God had blessed me with my gifts and had allowed my dream to come true, but that I had screwed everything up. It was such a puzzle. I hated me. I loved me. I knew I was a failure, yet I thought I deserved the best of everything. I knew I should think of others, but I wanted everything for myself.

What a sad, sad cliché to learn for myself that money and fame really didn't buy happiness! Yet the lesson didn't sink in. I thought that maybe more money would satisfy that inner craving. My salary wasn't bad until you looked at the NBA where guys were making three times what I was and playing two hundred fewer games.

I was doing some television appearances for the club in California and was driving from Los Angeles down to San Diego when I heard something crazy on the radio. The sportscaster said that the great NBA star, David Thompson, had been signed to a new contract calling for $800,000 a year. I knew that couldn't be. I switched stations to see if anyone else was saying the same. Sure enough, I heard it again.

I was not in a place convenient to pull off and find a phone, so I just drove on in frustration. When it came on yet again, I exited immediately and drove around looking for a phone. I called the office and talked to Stan, my agent who was now president of the Globetrotters. "Did you hear what David Thompson just signed for? He's getting $800,000. Stan, with what I'm doing, I'm underpaid, man. I'm coaching, training, drawing the crowds, playing three hundred games a year, doing promotion. I *am* the Globetrotters, and you know it. I got to have at least what Thompson is getting."

"Lark, Lark, slow down. No way Thompson is getting that much in straight salary. Maybe in bonuses for performance or in deferred dollars, but no way, forget it. They've got it wrong."

An hour later I heard it again, and this time it was explained. The $800,000 a year was cash on the barrel head.

I called Stan back. "Yes, he is! I want to renegotiate."

He promised. "We'll talk."

We met in Tampa the next week, and he explained that if they gave me even a hundred thousand more right then, it would throw their tax status off to the point where it would cost them hundreds of thousands more to do it. Even if I had believed him, it wouldn't have made any difference. I was thinking of me, not him, not the Trotters, nobody. In the end, I didn't believe he was sincere anyway.

"Lark, we'll give it to you on the other end, set you up for life."

I didn't trust anybody. "No. Cash. The club is making almost $20 million a year. You can pay me. And I want something for the years I was underpaid, too."

He said we would have to talk again.

I still tried to see my kids when I could. A year after Willye's and my divorce was final, I went to Connecticut to take my then high-school-age daughter, Beverly, to the hospital. She had a curvature of the spine that had to be straightened out, and she would be in a full body cast. The divorce and our concern over her ailment had torn the family apart.

Willye and I were formal with each other. I didn't hate her, but I could sense her bitterness. I was just sad when we had to interact. I still loved my children. And of course I was hurting for Beverly, even though I hadn't been around much to help out.

After I got her to the hospital and made sure everything was all right, I was going to pick up a lady friend and go to my mother's for my birthday dinner. It was April 25, 1978. In two days I would head for London, then a game in Germany and our annual European tour.

I was in downtown New York in a rented car, alone. Traffic was heavy. My car was tonked from behind. I didn't think much of it. I glanced in my rearview mirror. A black woman was backing up. I planned to ignore the tap. It happened all the time in bumper-to-bumper traffic. I hoped she wouldn't get out and expect me to, as well. There would be no damage worth worrying about.

But she wasn't getting out. She was coming at me again, this time fast! *Oh, no, this is someone who recognizes me and thinks she's going to get some publicity!* SMASH! I lurched around in the seat to stare at her. It was Willye! And she was backing up again! I dove from the car just before she rammed it again. I ran across the street to a policeman on the sidewalk and started to introduce myself.

"I know who you are, Meadowlark. What's the problem?"

"That's my former wife. We've been divorced over a year. Listen, I don't want any trouble. I don't want to press charges. I just want to get out of here."

"All right, sir. I'll come over with you to talk to her, and when I get her attention off you, you can slip away."

We hurried back across, and I waited by the door of my car. The policeman tried to soothe Willye, but she was pretty upset. When I thought she was distracted, I opened my door and started to step in. I heard her coming. All at once I felt like she had punched me in the back with her fist.

From the sidewalk I heard a voice. "She stabbed him!" I turned to look at the policeman. I could tell from the look on his face that the bystander was right. He looked like he didn't know whether to deal with Willye or me. He grabbed her and flagged down a squad car to take me to the hospital. "Don't try to take it out, buddy. Let 'em do that in emergency."

They told me it looked like a small steak knife. I was angry. I assumed she did it to embarrass me in the press. I knew there would be publicity, but I wasn't prepared for the magnitude or the immediacy of it. As I lay in the emergency room and a doctor cut off my new leather jacket, I joked that they should just pull the knife out and try to save the jacket. Then I saw the corridor fill up with press.

There wasn't much pain, and I didn't take the wound seriously, even though I was put in intensive care. I called friends to assure them I was okay, no matter what they might hear on the news. A couple of friends came to visit me, and the hospital staff tried to run them out. "You run them out, I'm going with them." They were allowed to stay a little longer.

In the morning I checked myself out of the hospital, with the promise that I would see a doctor right away. That's when I got scared. The doctor told me I shouldn't be walking and that if the knife had gone another half-inch into my body or farther on either side, I would have died. I remembered that telegram so many years ago. . . . "Deeply regret to inform you of your father's untimely passing due to accidental knife wound."

Before I left for London, and then Germany, I made sure everyone knew that I wasn't about to press charges. I don't know why

Willye did it, and I don't think I ever will. Maybe she doesn't know.

Regardless, I knew I was lucky to be alive. Still I would be putting myself in the line-up in London and playing as long as I could. The team was going to pot with me as the center of controversy, and I wasn't going to sit out and let them dethrone me.

26

Stabbed in the Back Again

I'm not comfortable kissing and telling or feuding and telling. It wasn't always that way. For the first several years following my painful separation from the Globetrotters, I was an angry, bitter man. I didn't mind telling people—not just anyone, of course— exactly what happened to me and who I felt was responsible.

For reasons that will become apparent, I'm no longer angry or bitter. I was hurt, betrayed by people I trusted, people I thought were my friends, and some of that pain remains. But I've been able to put aside the longings for revenge. No man can do that on his own.

I want to tell the story, to set the record straight, but I'm choosing not to name names of ballplayers. There would be no purpose served in opening old wounds, resurrecting old charges, rekindling old arguments over who really did or didn't say or do what. People would be hurt, and worse, families would be hurt. I don't want that.

The fact is that the start of the 1978 summer European tour was the beginning of the end of the relationship, and it would prove— grieved as I am to admit it—as painful as my divorce. In truth, it was a divorce. I spent more time with and for the Globetrotters over twenty-three years than I ever had with my family. I traveled almost constantly with them. Many said I *was* the Globetrotters, that you couldn't name another Globetrotter off the top of your head unless you'd just seen us in person or on TV, and then you might remember that bald guy they called Curly—Curly Neal.

I knew how important I was to the team, but under new ownership by Metromedia, a superstructure of new vice presidents and
managers had to flap its wings, each of its separate parts establish-
ing itself as a boss.

By now I was a coach, trainer, recruiter, star, and boss of the
team. It would have been fine with me if all the junior executives
and MBA's stayed at headquarters in Los Angeles and called me
in occasionally to tell me how we were doing financially. But each
wanted to be responsible for our success, to be my boss, to keep
me in my place.

They thought I was getting too big for my britches. I admit I
wasn't having the best relationship with all the players, and many
times I just met up with them on the court. I found my own ways
to and from the stadiums, and I had all kinds of personal appearances to make on the side.

I was conscientious about keeping drugs off the team. I roamed
the halls of the hotel at night so I knew who the guys were running
with and who had problems with alcohol. I was a teetotaler, but I
made the rounds of discos and nightclubs so I knew what was
going on.

I sensed the team getting away from me, but I felt that if I had
the backing of the home office, I could have kept the thing together and made it a success. The Globetrotter name was and is
the most well known in sports, and I felt I had had a lot to do with
that. I knew more about the team, the organization, the demands,
and the details than anyone at the time.

I knew I wasn't the ballplayer in my forties that I had been in
my twenties, but I was every bit the showman, and probably even
better. By now my timing was second nature, and I knew how to
"turn on" a crowd from the minute I stepped onto the floor. The
problems were off the court.

One of the complications was that besides being coach, I was
vice president of the players' union. So, when they began to mu-
tiny, it required complex maneuvering. They said they wanted a
meeting. I told them I'd call a meeting, but I wanted to protect
myself from getting into any trouble over grievances. I'll bring my
attorney, I told them, since I can't represent the players and management at the same time.

I called a meeting in a Holiday Inn in San Francisco following a game we played in Oakland. The ones who wanted it originally didn't show, but word got back to management that I had called a meeting and invited my personal representative.

That was seen as an attempt to start a strike, but I wasn't sure what had taken place. The players had been upset about getting too little rest and too much travel, violating their contracts. I said I would check it out.

To me, the show, the crowd, was still everything, in spite of my greed. You put on your best show, did your job right, settled for nothing short of excellence, were on time, showed some responsibility and discipline, and as long as you weren't getting walked on or taken advantage of, you made the best of it. That, too, made me a relic. Next thing I knew, management was upset with me for having called a meeting and getting things stirred up.

The night after I was stabbed in New York City, I started and played most of the game in London. I could tell from the looks on the players' faces that they were amazed I had even shown up. They were disappointed, too. "You okay, Lark?"

"Of course I'm okay. Let's go!"

"You need anybody to take over some of your reems tonight?"

"No! I'm ready."

Apparently, some had been practicing, dividing up the spoils, assigning each other the choice comedy bits. But I hadn't died, much to the dismay of many in the front office and on the bench. I know that sounds overstated, but I truly believe that many in the organization would have been relieved to have gotten rid of me so easily. The players had had enough of the grouchy old man who got lots of attention—on the court and off—and management knew I had gone over the brink when I started demanding a salary as big as the NBA's highest paid player.

Ironically, the stabbing made me more popular than ever. It was on the news and in the London papers, and the sympathy started on the plane ride over. By the time I hit the court, I received standing ovations and good wishes from everyone. Everyone except most of my teammates and my bosses. Stan Greeson had promised to talk to me again about my salary. I wanted it now.

For the past two summers, the Globetrotters had advertised in

England that it would be the last time Britons would get to see me play. Fair enough. I was at the age where it might have made sense for me to move into management or something else. But nothing had been formalized. I still had a multiyear deal. Worse, I was a threat to management because I wouldn't back down.

They considered me hard to deal with, and they began to promise different players that they would be the next lead clown. That was a serious mistake. For one thing, you can only have one, and I wasn't gone yet. Even if I had retired, what do you do with the two or three you have promised the spot? The maneuvering was obvious, and while I felt betrayed, I was more stubborn about staying.

I demanded a follow-up meeting with Greeson about my salary. I was taking enough heat from above and below that I wanted that one thing settled. Greeson came to London, but he had other plans. He wasn't there just to talk to me, but to talk to all the other players, too.

I didn't know about that. I was strong and pushy and told him I wasn't going to settle for less than $800,000 a year and a bonus equivalent to $50,000 a year for the twenty previous years in which I was underpaid. I had agreed privately with my lawyers that we would settle for as little as $500,000 in salary and $250,000 in make-up payments. Stan promised to go back to Metromedia to plead on my behalf. He made no promise except to try, but he had gathered damaging information about me from the players.

I didn't know it, but Metromedia had no intention of giving in to my salary demands. Their view was that I had a binding contract and that they were under no obligation whatever to renegotiate it. They were within their legal rights, of course. There was no recourse for me. But at the time, in the thick of the battle, I saw only my side.

I'm not saying that Metromedia didn't have an ethical obligation to pay me more. I still believe they did. But they held the trump cards. They didn't like my style, my attitude, my value to the business. They weren't going to budge, and it soon became clear that what they really wanted was out of the deal.

They hoped I'd crack, break down, take a swing at someone, quit, violate my contract. Meanwhile, they pushed me to give certain players more time on the court, in my position, doing my routines. They were shortsighted. They didn't realize that you can't replace someone overnight who has built a reputation over two decades. I'm not saying I was a legend, but there are many people who would say I was. And there are many who will say that the Globetrotters have never been the same without me.

But remember, at that time, I trusted Stan. He told me to hang in there, to keep doing what I was doing. We met one more time, this time in Spain, and he said he was working on it and would do the best he could for me. Meanwhile, I was to change nothing. I knew the players were upset, but I believed that management was somewhat behind me and that my new salary was at least in the works.

The European tour was becoming a real nightmare off the court. The fans turned out and loved us, and somehow I was able to put my personal problems aside and give my best show. But the players weren't happy. They wanted beer on the bus. They wanted their local women on the bus. They wanted beer in the locker room. They wanted to show up just in time for the game, wear their uniforms in hotel lobbies and in the stands before games, just for the notoriety. I said no. No beer on the bus or in the locker room. No bimboes on the bus. No wearing the uniform except on the court. And I wanted them in the locker room a half-hour before the game. Then I moved that up to an hour.

Management overruled me on beer in the locker room and on the bus after games. I should have seen the handwriting on the wall then. A couple of the players tried to set me up by requesting things I couldn't give them. One wanted me to have a doctor come and see him when he was sick. None would have come anyway, but I was made to look cheap because I advised him to go to the doctor instead.

Another faked a serious family problem that required him to return immediately to the States. While he was there, he did his best to confirm all the dirt Stan had dug up on me. When the ballplayer returned (just two weeks after Stan had told me to keep doing what I was doing and that he would tell Metromedia I deserved the raise), he slipped a letter to me from headquarters. I had been relieved of my coaching responsibilities, and another player was to take over.

I called a meeting of the players. I said, "I'm no longer your coach. I will continue to play and do what I'm told. But let me tell you something. They're trying to break us down. If they can get to me, the most well-known Globetrotter, they'll be coming after you, one by one. If you let this happen to me, you'll be next. I have a binding contract, so I'll be all right. But some of you will be easier victims."

I really shouldn't have expected any support from the players, but at that time I wasn't aware that they had done me in. They had tried to make me look bad on the court, firing passes at my feet, missing plays, and all that. I was prepared and flexible enough that I could make it all into a gag. But they told management that I couldn't play anymore (I've only been playing nine years since!) and that they couldn't play for me anymore. I was too tough, too demanding, too insensitive. They may have been right there, but I believed in doing things the old-fashioned way, the right way.

I never saw or heard from Stan Greeson again.

During the last two weeks of that European tour, I simply did my job. No one wanted to talk to me. I was given a few assignments to do some of my old reems, but mostly the new guys were taking their shots at it. Even though I had time left on my contract, clearly I was being pushed out.

When the season ended, we split up in France. I had never flown on the Concorde, so I booked the flight and flew to New York. It was an amazingly short trip, but I got a lot of thinking done. By the time we landed in New York, I was convinced I should leave, negotiate a settlement—with much of that going to lawyers, of course—and call it quits.

It wasn't an easy decision. I could hardly remember life before the Globetrotters. I had been encouraged to get into singing and acting, but I was scared of the prospect of life off the basketball court. What would I do? Should I follow through with it?

I immediately flew from New York to my new home in Los Angeles. By the time I got there, my mind was made up. There would be no turning back. I knew it would be hard. I didn't know how hard. (Nearly ten years later, I'm still referred to as a Globetrotter. Many people don't realize yet that I've left and have had two of my own teams since then. I get asked all the time how it is to play with the first woman Globetrotter. Someone always thinks they just saw me play with the Trotters on "Wide World of Sports.")

I guess down deep I still consider myself a Globetrotter. But the end was even nastier than I imagined it could be. Several of the players went to New York and New Jersey where they were interviewed on tape by lawyers who built a case against me as an incompetent player and coach. Some of the most staggering lies were that I was a druggie and a boozer. That's absolutely, categorically untrue, and anyone who said otherwise knows it. They also said I was a womanizer, which I can't deny, but there were precious few who weren't, especially among those who said I was.

This is the first time this story has been publicized. The things I'm saying here are the truth, and yet I love the Globetrotters. I always have. I always will. I hope I've made it clear where I was selfish and greedy and wrong, too. Frankly, nothing would make me happier than to somehow be hooked up with the Trotters again someday, in what role, I couldn't say.

I was scared, lonely, disappointed, worried, and relieved all at the same time. The only thing I saw on my horizon was a big question mark. One of the first things I wanted to do was talk to Wilt Chamberlain about his idea that I start my own team. He had been pushing me that way for a long time, but I knew I'd need his support and involvement for the best possibility of success. Meanwhile, I licked my wounds and tried to get used to being a *former* Harlem Globetrotter.

The relationship ended in the worst possible way. I almost felt like I was the former Meadowlark Lemon.

27

The Bucketeers

The anger in my gut didn't leave me, but I covered it with activity. I didn't even have time to enjoy the 16,000-acre cattle ranch I bought in Arizona. You'd have thought half the entertainment world had just been waiting for me to get off the crazy Globetrotter schedule so I could try other things.

The first thing I did was to costar as a basketball-playing preacher man with Philadelphia 76ers' superstar Julius "Dr. J." Erving in a funny film called *The Fish That Saved Pittsburgh.* If that doesn't sound like a title that would pull down an Academy Award, that's all right. It was reasonably successful, put some money in my pocket, and gave me a world of experience.

I felt like a rookie, yet my performance was applauded by critics. I was known as a Globetrotter, of course, but no one knew whether I could act in the more subtle comedic ways that work on the big screen or on TV. When the Globetrotters played on ABC's "Wide World of Sports," I caught the eyes of executives from all three networks.

I appeared in sitcoms, on talk and game shows, and in some pilots. I cut a record called "My Kids," which was also well received. I finally landed a regular spot on "Hello, Larry," starring McLean Stevenson. Again, I learned a lot. I played a retired basketball player who owned a sporting goods store and an apartment building in which the other characters lived.

We taped our show in a building at Metromedia Square, and I found Metromedia people avoiding me. I don't know if they were afraid of me or would have simply been embarrassed to run into me. Once I greeted three of them on the elevator. "How you guys doin'?" I was smiling.

They cringed. "Fine. And you?"

I nodded. "Fine."

"Good to see you."

I'll bet.

I was making good money for the fifty-two episodes over two years, besides a bundle for endorsements and commercials. The show was canceled after two years, one season short of being long enough for syndication, and almost one year short of my doubling my per-episode fee. But it had been a good run, and I enjoyed it.

I had lady friends, a nice apartment, a full schedule, and to most would have seemed on top of the world. But I missed basketball. At least, that's what I thought I missed.

One day I was talking with Andy Johnson and Wilt Chamberlain as we were sitting on the curb in front of the University of California at Los Angeles. We had dreamed of our own comedy basketball team, one that would do what the Globetrotters used to do and what they had failed to do—we felt—since I left them.

Wilt had an idea. A big one, as usual. "Let's call them the Galactics!"

I laughed. "No way, man."

"You want me to play, you'll call 'em the Galactics! Why watch the Globetrotters when you can watch the Galactics?" That twinkle was in his eye.

We played with several other names. I was in a quiet mood. "How 'bout just the Bucketeers?"

Andy nodded. " 'S'long as you play, Lark, it don't make much difference what we call ourselves."

Wilt raised his eyebrows. "Meadowlark Lemon's Bucketeers."

The name stuck. I had to wait a few years until after my contract with the Trotters terminated, because it carried a noncompeting clause. Once I was free, I was eager to get rolling. Okay, I didn't know what I was doing. What else was new? I still hadn't learned my lesson. I trusted people.

It took three long seasons of ups and downs, but the Bucketeers flopped. There's no gentle way of saying it. Andy refereed and played when I desperately needed him. Wilt played in the big games, the TV games, as we had agreed. And he said nice things. He told an interviewer that he had started his career with me and he wanted to end it with me, too.

Those guys were great. Other team members were good, too—some former Trotters, a lot of young talent. The problem was, the team was mine, and we were undercapitalized. That's a nice way of saying that I didn't have enough money to carry it myself.

It's expensive to put a team on the road, but we had a good one, the best in talent and comedy on the circuit in my opinion, and I should know. I chose the wrong promoters, plain and simple. They had done a decent job with my other endeavors, but their hearts were in rock 'n' roll promoting. Our offices were in Century City, which is pretty uptown in the entertainment industry. I think that location was more for the benefit of the rock side of their business because for a long time, the Bucketeers were carrying them financially, and the rent was pretty steep.

The first few months were all right, but then things started to sour. We were short of marketing and management help, and most of all, we were short of cash. In the midst of the hassle of getting uniforms designed and made, I met someone who made a small impression on me, but whose ultimate importance to me I could never have measured.

Heidi Rasnow was a young costume designer who worked out of her home. She inherited the project of making our Bucketeer uniforms from another designer who just couldn't handle it. Heidi had a week to sew a dozen uniforms with no measurements. All she knew was that most of the ballplayers were giants, and that one was Wilt Chamberlain, a seven-footer. She was asking questions like "How big is the chest of a person who is two feet taller than I am?"

I had designed the uniforms, and the team bore my name, so given the time crunch, I was elected to visit her. When I got to her house, she had fabric spread all over the living room floor. I stood in the doorway, smiling at the little Jewish girl. She spoke first. "Do you know how to leap?"

"Yeah. Why?"

" 'Cause that's the only way you're going to get in here."

I leaped over the fabric and shook her hand. "Meadowlark Lemon."

"Meadowlake?"

"Meadowlark."

"Oh, and you used to be with the Globetrotters?"

I nodded.

"My family used to love to watch you guys on TV, but I never knew any of the names. Whoever it was who did most of the funny stuff, he was brilliant."

I smiled but didn't own up to it. It was refreshing to meet someone who didn't know who I was, who wasn't treating me like a star or a personality, but who appreciated my talent without even knowing it.

She sent me to the bathroom to try on my uniform. It looked like a Renaissance piece, very colorful, with a plumed hat. She nodded when I appeared, but I wanted to know the truth. "What do you think of it?"

"The truth?"

"Of course."

"To be honest with you, the concept is great, but the outfits stink."

How long had it been since someone told me the truth? I told her to keep going.

"You can't move in them. They don't look good. The fabrics are wrong. I'm sewing them up, if that's what you want, but I won't be putting my label in them because I don't want the credit for them."

I had known from the moment I put the uniform on that it wasn't right. It was fun, exciting almost, to see my concept in living color. But she was right. It was uncomfortable and confining, and the material was unlike anything I'd ever worn on the court. I felt like I was wearing someone's living room drapes.

"What would you do about them, Heidi?"

"I'd have to work around the clock to meet your schedule, but I'd start from scratch. Redesign them. Choose better fabrics, different patterns. I'd need all the measurements, of course."

"If I could get you that, do you know someone who could handle the redesign?"

"I could do that."

"What about doing the patterns?"

"I could do that."

"What about getting the fabric and sewing them?"

"I could do that, too."

"Is there anything you can't do?"

"Plenty, believe me. But I'm willing to take on this challenge."

And she did take it on. Later she would have to redo all of them for an "NBC Sportsworld" special, and Heidi and I became good friends. We worked a lot together, and I admired her. She was honest to the point of being blunt, something I longed for in people. Plus, she was good. She knew what she was capable of doing, and she did it.

The Bucketeers were getting good television coverage, but our managers didn't know how best to promote us. I was hot, well received, and in demand. And when we had Wilt with us, he was a big draw. Right at the time we should have been making the most of it, my partners were promoting rock acts, not sure what to do with us. Managing a sports franchise is a specialized thing, not just another assignment for a big booking agency.

I made mistakes, too. I took on people who were between jobs, offered them big salaries, and then saw them sue me when we were late with a paycheck or two. I know that paying late puts a hardship on people, and I hated to do it. We always paid as soon as we could, and the people were making more than they would have elsewhere.

A promoter sold me on letting him promote a block of our games. Although he was young, he had a good presentation, so we signed with him. He guaranteed us $7,500 per game. Thirty-some games later, he owed us $250,000 and was nowhere to be found. I started paying the bills myself.

A man from the East who claimed to be a "jack-of-all-trades"—agent/fundraiser/manager—wanted to manage me. He said he was going to raise $5.5 million to put the Bucketeers on easy street, pay our bills, give us room to breathe, to expand. Sounded good. But every time I talked to him, the figure he was going to raise dwindled a little. Then a lot. Finally, he was going to raise

$300,000. I know he got $100,000 from one group of investors and about $50,000 from another.

During that time, I thought there was money in the bank. I wrote checks to lease our bus from a company in Florida. When we returned, there was a warrant out for my arrest on a bad check charge. Again, the payback had to come from my own pockets, which were wearing mighty thin.

The team played on television several times, once in Harlem, once on an aircraft carrier in San Diego, once at Epcot Center. We also played at my daughter's high school in Fairfield, Connecticut, which was a special treat for me. My kids had begun to forgive and forget all the divorce troubles, and now I could see them mature.

I was prey to bad people who looked for successful people, naive in business. Projects failed without my knowing why, but I was blamed. I kept trying to tell myself I made a better boss for myself than anyone I had worked for before. But it seemed a new crisis would arise daily, and Meadowlark would be digging deep to keep from going bankrupt.

Heidi was aware of a lot before I was. People thought that she was a dumb little designer and that they could say anything they wanted in front of her and she wouldn't know what was going on.

Heidi knew I was blind about some of my associates. She tried to warn me, but I didn't know what to think. What business was it of hers? I hardly knew her. She was a mere child, bad-mouthing my business ability. "I'll handle it, Heidi. Don't worry about it."

"Your friends are not your friends, Meadowlark. Be careful."

I resented that input. It bothered me, much like it bothered me when she tried to tell me about God. Here she was, Jewish, and she was talking about being born again and being a Christian and having Jesus in her life. I was polite, but that stuff was too much for me. I didn't want any part of it. It made me nervous.

God was all right. I knew He was up there somewhere, and I figured He was part of everybody and everybody was part of Him. Ballplayers and others in the past had said similar things, but I wasn't listening. Religion was personal and private, and in my opinion it was each to his own. She tried to tell me that Jesus wasn't a religion, He was a person. I was blind and deaf to it. It made no sense to me.

During the Christmas holidays of 1981, I had narrowly avoided getting roped into a Bible study, of all things. An old girlfriend invited me to what I thought was just a Christmas party at the home of some friends of mine. Eula McClaney and her daughters, Burnestine and LaDoris, had been friends of professional athletes for years and often fed the stars when they came to town.

I always enjoyed their company, so I quickly agreed to go. When we got there, we walked in on a group of people with Bibles in their laps, smiles on their faces, and prayer on their lips. What a deal! Get invited to a party and it turns out it's also something else. I kept right on moving, straight to the banquet table where I busied myself, creating a plate of food.

Soon, whatever had been going on in the other room broke up and everyone gathered around for dinner. After dinner, Burnestine introduced me to a tall, skinny friend of hers named Lorelei. I had noticed her when she walked in because she was kind of cool.

Anyway, neither Lorelei nor I was impressed with the other. We were introduced on a first-name basis, and she assumed my old girlfriend was my wife. She had never heard of me, and she wasn't my type, so I didn't give her another thought until several months later.

Meanwhile, my business woes with the Bucketeers continued. I had been told that all the bills were paid, including Heidi's, so when I returned to the news that she had brought an action against the Bucketeers through Dun and Bradstreet, I was livid. I had enough problems in my life, trying to run a business that was quickly going broke. I didn't need someone who called me her friend adding this insult. I dialed her number, and as soon as Heidi answered, I let her have it. I mean, I didn't pause for a breath. I only said one thing printable, "You call yourself a Christian. . . ."

I was vile. She didn't say a word. Not one word in her own

defense. Nothing. That fried me. I knew I had her. When I said my piece, and repeated much of it a time or two, I slammed the phone down. I was on my way out for a two-week trip, and I was glad to be going. The last thing I wanted to do was talk to her again. Ever.

28

"Call Heidi!"

On that two-week road trip early in 1982, I was hit with more problems. The Bucketeers were falling apart around me. Bills piled up, threats came. I began to assess my assets, and I realized that I was going to go down with the ship.

I'm basically an optimist. I had put my previous troubles behind me and kept looking for new adventures, new plans to hit it big, to stay famous, to make money, to be a success. It would be hard to match my popularity as a Globetrotter, but my hope was to parlay that fame into bigger and better things in television and with this new team.

Again, my plans were unraveling, and there seemed to be nothing I could do about it. I'm a private person but not too reflective. I don't generally mope about failure or disappointment, but this was getting to me. Some old wounds were still open, and now I realized I was failing in a big way.

Now, just as with the Globetrotters, I had counted on people. People had always let me down. I had made my own mistakes, sure, but I would never treat a dog the way I had been treated.

I had filled life with everything I thought would make a man happy: things, money, fame, security, work, busy-ness. Still, I wasn't happy. I was frustrated, disillusioned. My resources, both financial and psychological, were depleted.

I had nowhere to turn. The Catholic faith I had embraced as a child—just because my friends had been into it—had long since become a memory. I believed in God. He was okay with me. I tried to be a decent enough guy, hoping He would look upon me with favor.

When I returned to L.A., I realized I was also out of friends. Clearly, our management was being ripped off. I didn't know the full extent of it yet, but I was getting an idea. I knew how low I was when I found myself sitting on my bed, listing on a yellow pad some of the mistakes I'd made over the years.

I was only going to jot a short list, but things kept crashing through my mind. I remembered not only what I had done wrong, but also that something inside me had, in essence, warned me against teaming up with certain people or making certain investments. I had been so busy, I wasn't listening. I wasn't into the supernatural, so I figured whatever that feeling or voice was, it had to be in my mind.

As I was going through that depressing exercise, I was impressed so deeply within that it was almost like I heard an audible voice. I know I didn't, but these words were so clearly laid upon my heart that I felt I heard them: "Call Heidi. Call Heidi. Call Heidi."

I thought I was going crazy. Maybe it was all the activity of remembering my faults and reminding myself of that voice inside me that was causing me to hear things. Anyway, not two weeks before, I had cussed Heidi so bad, I knew I'd never see, hear from, or talk to her again as long as I lived.

"Call Heidi. Call Heidi."

I shook my head. "That's crazy. I can't do it."

"Call Heidi."

I didn't want to hear it again. I called Heidi.

"Heidi? Meadowlark!" I tried to sound like my jovial old self so she would know all was forgiven and forgotten. I didn't know why she had to come after me for money when I had been told she had been paid, but for now, I was just obeying a voice.

There was silence on the other end, but I knew she hadn't hung up. She was listening.

"How ya doin', Heidi?"

Nothing.

"Listen, I just got back in town, and I wanted to call you."

Silence.

"I, uh, I'm just so sorry for the way I acted. Please forgive me."
I must have hurt her deeply. Still, she didn't respond. "That's all
I've got to say, Heidi. I understand if you're still upset, but I want
you to know I apologize and want your forgiveness."

Maybe I should have been offended that she still wouldn't say
anything. But I wasn't thinking that way. I just felt sorry.
Ashamed. "I'll be seeing you, Heidi. Bye."

She said nothing. I hung up softly.

Immediately, I was impressed to call her again. "Call Heidi.
Call Heidi."

Now I knew I was going nuts. "I just called her!"

"Call Heidi."

"She obviously doesn't want to talk to me."

"Call Heidi."

I dialed. "Heidi. It's me again. Listen, we've been friends a
long time. I don't want this to come between us. I want to come
over to talk to you. Can I do that?"

I waited and waited for a response. Finally, it came. "Okay." It
wasn't cold, it wasn't unkind. She had thought about it, and it
was okay for me to come over. I didn't tell her when I would be
there, but the timing turned out right.

Early that afternoon a young friend of hers, a minister named
Jay, showed up at her studio. "Hi! What're you doing here?"

He smiled with a puzzled look. "I'm not sure. I never come
here."

She was glad to see him, but also puzzled. "So, what can I do
for you?"

Jay laughed, almost embarrassed. "I don't know. I just feel like
I'm supposed to be here."

Things like that aren't so unusual in Heidi's life. She had been
sharing her faith with every client since I met her. I had been
running the other way, but I knew a lot of people, dozens in fact,
had become converted right there in that studio.

Because of a couple of well-timed projects Heidi had to super-
vise just then, Jay had to cool his heels a few minutes before she
could get back to him. When I arrived, some piano movers had
just shown up, and she had to help them for a while.

I don't know what she saw when I came through that door, but

I could tell by the look on Heidi's face that she loved me and cared about me and that I must have looked like I had lost my last friend. She didn't have time for small talk. She didn't give me a chance to apologize in person. She simply jumped right to the heart of the matter, as always. "Meadowlark, I know what you need. You need Jesus."

Right between the eyes. So plain, so simple, so direct. I needed Jesus. She knew it. I knew it. That little voice that had told me to call her knew it. God knew it. He had sent that minister friend to be there just then. He had even sent distractions to keep Jay there. I could hardly speak, but I managed to whisper, "Okay. I'm ready."

She took me aside. "Can we pray for you and with you?"

"If you want to."

Jay explained to me that Jesus Christ had paid for my sin. That sounded good to me. I understood that I was a sinner. He told me that I could become a true Christian and be saved from my sin, assured of heaven, and become born again, the way Jesus talked about in the New Testament, if I just asked God. I told him I wanted to.

He led me in a prayer, and I repeated it. "Dear God, I know I'm a sinner and that I need forgiveness. I believe Jesus died for me and will be my Savior if I receive Him as my Lord. Thank You for saving me and giving me eternal life."

I believed it and meant it as much as I understood those words at that time, but I must say that I left Heidi's house a little confused. It wasn't Heidi's fault. It wasn't Jay's fault. In fact, I believe they loved me into the kingdom of God. But they also assured me that I couldn't lose my salvation. I was assured of God's love and of eternal life, no matter what.

They weren't giving me a license to sin. Had they known how little background and training I'd had in church, they would have cautioned me not to sin just to prove I was already forgiven. I should have been established in a solid church, gotten into the Word every day, and started growing. But I took that assurance of my salvation and used it to do what I wanted.

I wish I could say my life changed that instant, but it didn't. I believe I was saved because I had been sincere and I had believed

God and received Christ. But for the next year, while I searched for a closer relationship to God by attending church here and there, I was still living like the old Meadowlark.

It was a tough time for me. It's hard to go from being number one in your own life to taking a back seat to Jesus Christ. The Bucketeers were fading fast. I was in debt up to my eyeballs. I couldn't make it all make sense. Here I had given myself to God, yet I was still in financial ruin. How did that jibe?

While I was in the middle of my spiritual struggle, Burnie McClaney called me. "Hey, I want you to talk to one of my girlfriends. Hang on."

Burnie was such a character! I decided to turn on the charm just for her. "Hello?"

"Hi! This is Lorelei."

It was the girl Burnie had introduced me to at Christmas. I remembered that I had not been overly impressed. Lorelei was not the typical curvaceous female. She was attractive, tall and thin, but I had been so carnal before that I determined whether a woman was my type or not just by looking at her.

And Lorelei was not my type. Still, because I liked Burnie so much, I joked with the girl for a few minutes and said I might call her again. I didn't know that God had begun working in her life, too. She didn't know it either. All she knew was that her world was being shaken.

She'd been a Christian since childhood and devout until she was eighteen. Then she went off to college and got involved in many things most kids get involved in. By the time I met her, she says she was completely away from the Lord and living in the world.

Recently, however, many things had changed in her life. Her sister, Corliss, one she had partied and hung out with, had started attending the Crenshaw Christian Center, where Dr. Frederick Price was pastor. She had returned to her faith and was so apt to say "Praise the Lord," that Lorelei and the rest of the family started using that as her nickname. "Have you talked with 'Praise the Lord' lately?"

Lorelei was suspicious of any flamboyant pastor of a big church where many people were getting their lives changed. To her it smacked of Jim Jones and The People's Temple and she vowed Fred Price would never get her. She would never set foot in that church.

Then, not long after Lorelei had enjoyed "one of our wildest parties ever" with several friends who had been close since junior high days, one of the guys announced that he had been born again and was back in church. She wondered what was happening. This boy had been like a brother to her for years, yet he had made this big decision without even discussing it with her. Next thing she knew, he was engaged, and he hadn't talked to her about that either.

First my sister, now my old friend. What's happening to all these people? she wondered. *They're not going to be my friends anymore.*

It was right about that time that I called her and we started seeing each other. When I told her I'd been born again, she thought the whole world was ganging up on her. Even though it had been many years since she was serious about her faith and she was struggling now, she could tell immediately what was wrong in my life. She suggested that I get away and log some time in the Bible, memorizing Scripture and praying.

I should have, but I didn't. Clearly, the Holy Spirit was working on me because I felt bad when I lived for myself. But I didn't seem to have the strength to change. I was impressed to keep striving, but for about a year, I floated spiritually. I filled voids with things just as I always had, but I knew something was wrong. Something was missing.

One ironic development was that Heidi explained she was dropping her suit against the club for the nearly ten thousand dollars we owed her. I had discovered that indeed she had been a victim, too, and that we did owe her the money. I had to ask, "Why would you write that off?"

"Now that you've become a Christian, you're my brother. The Bible is clear that we are not to sue our brothers."

That hit hard. Leading me to Christ had cost her in a big way. I still wanted to pay her. I wanted to pay everyone off. I was in a bad way. I had a power source I wasn't tapping.

Heidi told me I needed to talk with the pastor of Crenshaw Christian Center, Dr. Fred Price. She called and made an appointment for me, and suddenly, I was as nervous as I had been in years. I didn't know what to expect.

I don't know what it was, but maybe I had a superstitious view of pastors. Or maybe I thought he would try to hit me up for money the way a lot of clergy do. I dreaded the meeting, but I had to go through with it. I wanted help. I had been a Christian for a year, yet I wasn't getting anywhere. I knew I should see a change in my life, but I didn't see much.

Fred Price put me at ease right away. I told him my troubles, how I had finally become aware of the void in my life, ironically *after* I had become a Christian. He was direct, friendly, warm, loving. And he talked straight with me, just like Heidi had. "The things you want to do, you can't do 'em anymore. They got to die. That old Meadowlark Lemon was crucified. He's gone. You're a new creature in Christ. You don't need a preacher, you need a teacher. And you've come to the right place."

From the first Sunday, I was hooked. The Reverend Price was a dynamic preacher. But what he really did was to teach. Straight from the Bible, no pulled punches. Lots of solid, down-to-earth doctrine. How to live. How to get Scripture into your life. I got into the Bible every day. I listened to tapes by Price and many other Christian leaders. I read Christian books.

I remembered how I had slept with a basketball as a youngster learning the game. Now, when I go to a hotel room, the first thing I do before unpacking anything else is set my Bible and my notes and my tape recorder on the bed. That's where they are stored for when I need them early in the morning or in the middle of the day or just before I go to sleep. I'm into it, man, and once I got into it, my life changed.

29

Last Words

Lorelei and I had been seeing each other, not exclusively, for almost a year. She was going to Crenshaw Christian Center with me, something she had said she would never do. One Sunday, when we visited the church of her old friend—the one who had become a Christian and had gotten married without consulting her—she recommitted her life to God.

I was seeing other women at that time, too, and by this time I was in love with someone I had been seeing for years, a woman from New York I had just led to Christ. I thought if I got married again, she would be the one.

Lorelei was articulate, smart, analytical, a real estate agent, successful. And now she was spiritual, too. She was sympathetic to what had happened to me in business and had begun to help out. Soon she was handling a lot of the office work, at first as a volunteer, just because she was a friend who cared.

When the office work began to leave her less and less time for her own business, I put her on the payroll. She was someone I trusted, someone who was honest. She was organized and started virtually running my business the right way for the first time since I left the Globetrotters. I began to depend upon her totally.

In love with her? I didn't even know it. Didn't think about it. We teased each other a lot, and more than once she said, "You're going to wind up marrying me." And I would laugh.

With her help, I finally started tying up all the loose strings in the failure of the Bucketeers. There were legal and financial hassles that I never could have handled alone. I wanted to start a new team, the Shooting Stars, where I would serve as coach and star and have a lot of say, but where someone else, someone I trusted, would put up the money, take the responsibility. Lorelei helped get that off the ground.

I didn't realize how close we'd grown, how dependent upon her I had become over a couple of years of working together. I still thought I was in love with someone else. And Lorelei was still teasing that someday I would marry her. Then one night on Christian television, right while I was being interviewed live, that little voice spoke to me. Suddenly, a statement burst from me. "I'm going to be married."

I almost laughed out loud. I wanted to apologize, to say I didn't even know why I said that. The host looked shocked, and before either of us could cover for my outburst, it came out again. "I'm getting married."

"You are?"

"Yes, I am."

"Well, who's the lucky lady?"

"She's sitting right there." I pointed at Lorelei in the audience. She was as shocked as I was, since we hadn't talked seriously about it and I certainly had never proposed. But she took it in stride. She had been serious when I thought she was teasing. She knew it would happen, and when it was announced, even in that offbeat way, it was confirmed for her.

We were married on September 20, 1985, at the McClaney home, and I have seen what marriage was meant to be. It was at Crenshaw Christian Center that I first saw that people could be happily married, that marriages could grow in Christ, that people could grow together. I wanted that. And that's what Lorelei and I have.

The things God has done for me since I received Christ would make a whole other book. Most amazing, I think, is that my entire family—all five kids and my former wife—became Christians the same year I did. They were all in different locations, all under different circumstances, but it happened to each one.

I have a better relationship with my kids than ever. Some who harbored bitterness have forgiven me, and they understand my side of the situation better now, too. At one point I visited Willye's home church in Atlanta, and with her in the audience, I publicly apologized for all the pain I had caused her. After church, we went out to lunch with a few relatives. There is still a lot of tension between us, and things will never be the same, of course, but we are civil to each other and we see each other as brother and sister in Christ.

I also called many other people from my past to ask their forgiveness for the feelings of bitterness and anger and even hatred I had felt toward them. I was able to share Scripture with them, and many of them asked my forgiveness, too. The Bible is clear that we cannot be forgiven of God if we are unwilling to forgive others. When I started doing that, a great weight was lifted off my shoulders.

Finally, God delivered me from the deep resentment I had harbored over the Globetrotter and Bucketeer situations. My new team, the Shooting Stars, got off to a good start, becoming ambassadors of the White House in Nancy Reagan's fight against drugs and setting up a nationwide tour. We speak in local schools on the evils of drugs, then we play a game where we also talk at half time about the same thing.

Recently, I visited my hometown and rapped with some of the old buddies you've been reading about in this book. I had shared Christ with several of them by phone during the months before, but this trip was just to reminisce and to refresh myself about the old neighborhood before getting started on this book.

We had a great time, laughing, teasing each other, and telling tall tales about each other. For several hours we just enjoyed each other's company at the Boys' Club.

One of the guys, Bunny, had rapped with us the night before but couldn't join us at the club that morning. He called from his office just before we finished. "Meadow, we were talkin' last night about Son and how he died a couple of years ago. I miss him, man, and I never got a chance to tell him I loved him. We never know when our time is gonna come, and I don't want anything to happen to you or to the rest of the Hometown Boys without me gettin' a chance to tell you I love you. We're always worryin' about bein' macho and not showin' our true feelin's, but I want you guys to know how I feel and I'm sorry I can't be there to tell you in person."

I shared that with the others, and we expressed our love to each other as we left the Boys' Club. They had to get back to work, and I had a plane to catch. It was such a warm and special time, we didn't want it to end.

Outside we stood with our shoulders hunched against a cold drizzle, and my old friends asked me more about how I got into the ministry. I knew they were really asking about how I got serious about my faith. They knew me. They knew my life. They had seen a dramatic change they found hard to believe. I think they wanted to know if it was real. I ran down the story the quickest way I knew how. When I started talking about how God had delivered me from skirt chasing, I could tell I was hitting close to home.

We said our good-byes. As we were getting into our cars in a light rain, one of the guys turned to me and said, "I'd like to rap with you about that."

Another chimed in, "Yeah, 'cause we're not kids anymore. I'm over fifty, you know. We got to get on the right side."

I made a promise. "I'll call you before I leave town." We raised fists at each other, and the two who had mentioned talking more drove off just ahead of us. As we pulled away from the curb, knowing they would be turning one way and we the other just a few blocks up the street, I realized I wouldn't have time to call them. They were clearly ready. When they noticed we had turned their way instead of toward the airport, they pulled over to see what was up. I jogged to their tiny car and wedged myself into the back seat, my knees pressing painfully on the back of the front seat.

"Listen, guys, I'm leavin', and there's not gonna be time for us to talk again. But, you know, you can have what I've got in just a few minutes. Is that what you want?"

They both nodded. "Exactly."

"That's right."

"Then will you say a little prayer with me?" They nodded

again. And I led them in the prayer that Heidi's friend prayed with me. I know they've got a long way to go. They need to get into the Word and into a good church and encourage each other. But I also know their lives have been changed, their souls have been saved.

And that's what it's all about.